ARCHITECTURAL
GUIDES FOR TRAVELERS

·

CHATEAUX
OF THE LOIRE

ARCHITECTURAL
GUIDES FOR TRAVELERS

•

CHATEAUX OF THE LOIRE

MARCUS BINNEY

CHRONICLE BOOKS • SAN FRANCISCO

First published in the United States in 1992 by Chronicle Books.

Series conceived by Georgina Harding
Editors: Elizabeth Haldane and Louisa McDonnell
Series design: Clare Finlaison
Design: Wendy Bann
Maps and plans: David Woodroffe
Picture research: Nicholas Shaddick
Index: Hilary Bird

Printed in England by Jolly & Barber Ltd., Rugby, Warks

Library of Congress Cataloging-in-Publication Data
Binney, Marcus.
    Chateaux of the Loire / by Marcus Binney.
      p. cm. – (Architectural guides for travelers)
    Includes bibliographical references and index.
    ISBN 0–87701–851–0 (pbk.)
      1. Loire River Valley (France)–Description and travel–Guide-
books. 2. Castles–France–Loire River Valley–Pictorial works.
3. Architecture–France–Loire River Valley–Guide-books.
I. Title. II. Series.
DC611.L81B55 1992
914.4'504839--dc20   91–30325
                                                CIP

10 9 8 7 6 5 4 3 2 1

Chronicle Books
275 Fifth Street
San Francisco, California 94103

CONTENTS

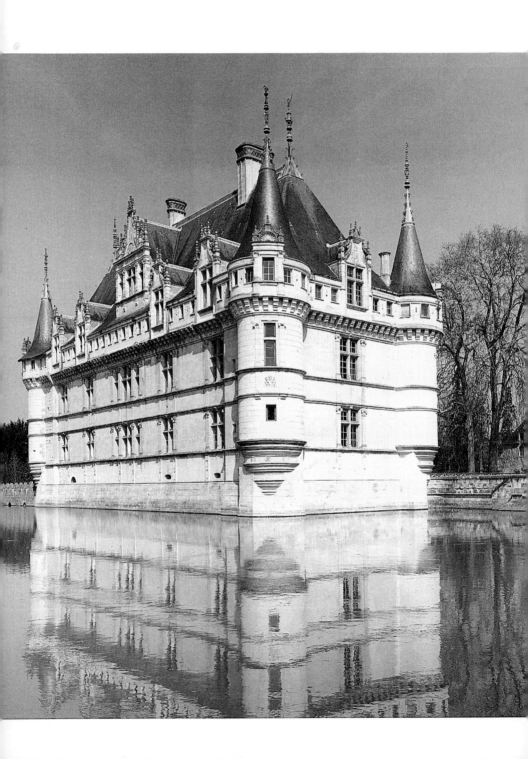

PREFACE

A new generation of owners and curators is breathing
fresh life and interest into the châteaux of the Loire.
These houses and castles are more renowned and
visited than the castles of Bavaria or the villas of the
Veneto. But in the past too many visitors have left
stultified by a surfeit of deadly guided tours through
barely furnished rooms.

Yet the overwhelming majority of Loire châteaux
are not in the hands of the state—and nowhere in
Europe are owners so wholly committed to public
opening. The key to enjoyment is to mix the famous
royal châteaux, which are inevitably thronged with
visitors, with the smaller less-frequented ones.

Numerous guidebooks already exist to the Loire
châteaux, but relatively few look in serious detail at
the architecture. Yet in the last few years there has
been a Renaissance in French architectural history,
with a fresh look being taken at the architecture of all
periods in the light of detailed studies of documenta-
tion. Substantial contributions have also been made
by English and American scholars.

Interest has spread to cover not only the
architecture but interiors, furnishings and gardens,
and the way the houses were used. While there is a
wealth of fascinating material on some châteaux, for
others there is remarkably little literature, let alone of
recent date. In each entry I have tried, as far as
possible, to set out the evolution of the building,
saying for whom it was built and when. In describing
the buildings I have indicated the places that I find
most sympathetically looked after, displayed and
restored. But all such impressions are to some extent
personal and enjoyment can depend on factors like the
weather and the crowds.

I have made a selection of some of the lesser-known
châteaux which can be visited, but there are many
more that cannot be included in a relatively short
guidebook, and part of the pleasure of a trip to the

(Opposite) Azay-le-
Rideau: the early
16th-century château
from across the moat.

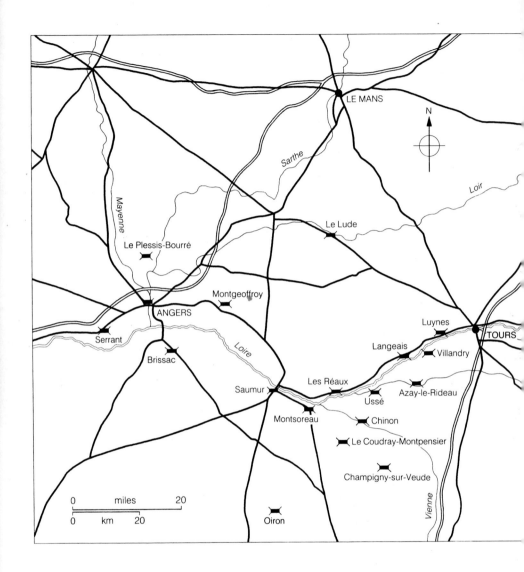

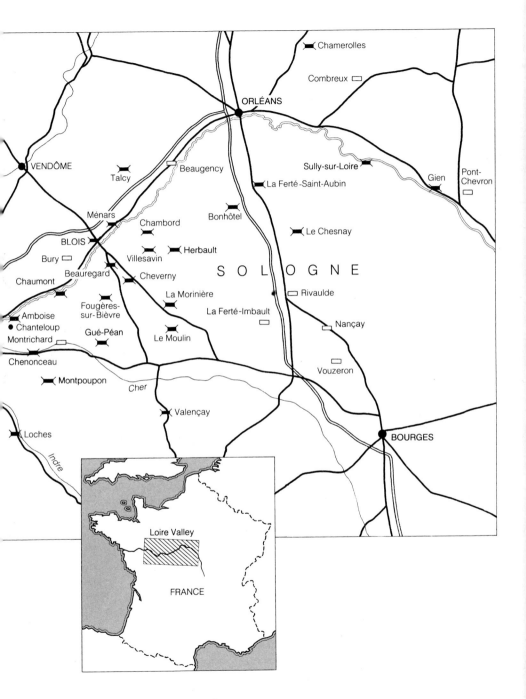

Loire is to search out additional small châteaux for yourself. There are not dozens to be visited, but hundreds, enough not just for one week or two, but a series of holidays based on different parts of the Loire Valley.

Using this guide

I have assumed that anyone using this guide will be equipped with a standard Michelin road map on which virtually every château described is marked. The better-known châteaux are marked with a black rectangle; lesser-known ones by a white rectangle edged in black. The Michelin maps are readily available, and come in atlas form for the whole of France. Easier to handle are the new large-size maps: the relevant ones are **Pays de Loire (232)** and **Centre Berry-Nivernais (238).** A small portion of the area north of Orléans is on **Paris et Environs (237).** In addition the Red Michelin Guide *France*, has excellent town maps with incoming roads numbered to link up with the regional maps. The map on pages viii and ix of this book shows all the châteaux described.

Opening times

A very large proportion of châteaux in the Loire Valley are regularly open, some all the year round, some only in summer. However the opening hours change from one month to another; therefore, in order not to be disappointed, obtain a copy of the lists of opening times—for addresses see p. 145.

Most châteaux are closed for two hours at lunch time, so if you want to see as much as possible try and arrive at your first château at the time of opening which may be the time of the first guided tour. Miss this and you can lose the best part of an hour. Where opening times are given as 9.30/11.15h, 11.15 indicates the start of the last guided tour of the morning. But beware: the closing time at the end of the day may indeed be just that, not the time of last admission.

INTRODUCTION

The builders

The Loire is promoted today as a 'valley of kings', but the builders of its earliest castles were in fact the warring counts of Anjou, Tours, Blois and Orléans. (France was not to become a territorial unity until the end of the reign of Louis XI, 1461–83). The most formidable of these feudal lords was the infamous **Fulk Nerra,** the Black Falcon, Count of Anjou (987–1040). He built a series of about 20 *donjons* (keeps) to consolidate his conquest of Touraine— they include those at Montrichard, Langeais and Loches.

Then came a period of English influence. Henry Plantaganet, Count of Anjou, succeeded to the English throne as Henry II in 1154. By the end of his reign, through inheritance, his marriage to Eleanor of Aquitaine, and his own energetic leadership, he controlled half France. He greatly improved the defences of the *château fort* (fortified castle) at Chinon, which lay at the heart of his French territory, and he died there in 1189. French fortunes revived markedly when, in 1202, King John lost Anjou to King Philippe Auguste of France. During the Hundred Years War, which began in 1337 as a result of the English claim to the French throne, numerous châteaux were damaged by the English. However, it was in the Loire Valley that, later on, the expulsion of the English began in earnest. At Chinon in 1429, Joan of Arc, the Maid of Orléans at last secured her audience with the future Charles VII and told him of her vision that she had been chosen by God to drive the English from France.

In 1453 the English were finally expelled and from then on the Loire Valley increasingly became the centre of French court life. Châteaux were now not so much defensive fortresses, as splendid residences for courtiers and kings. **Louis XI** (1461–83) greatly strengthened Langeais; **Charles VIII** (1483–98) carried out vast building works at Amboise; following Charles' death **Louis XII** (1498–1515) moved the court to Blois and immediately began building. **François I** (1515–47), following his accession (seven years after Henry VIII ascended the English throne), began the great Renaissance wing at Blois and in 1519 embarked on his magnificent palace at Chambord.

Many of the finest 15th- and 16th-century châteaux were built by courtiers and royal financiers. These houses were used as country residences; most of their owners already had handsome town houses in Blois, Tours or Orléans. Montsoreau rose in 1440–5 for Jean de Chambes, Counsellor of Charles VII. Le Plessis-Bourré was built in 1468–73 for Jean Bourré, treasurer to Louis XI. Philippe du Moulin, builder of the

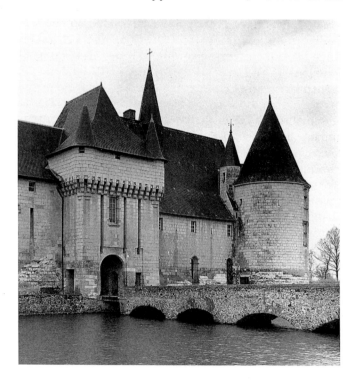

Le Plessis-Bourré: the gatehouse.

Château du Moulin, accompanied Charles VIII to Italy and was appointed chamberlain on his return. Jacques d'Espinay, at Ussé, was a chamberlain of Louis XII. Charles II d'Amboise, who completed the major part of Chaumont, was Grand Maître de la Maison du Roi and was appointed Governor of Milan by Louis XII. Three of the most important early Renaissance châteaux were built for wealthy bourgeois who held important positions at court. The Château de Bury (1511–24) was the work of Florimond Robertet, Secretary of Finances under Charles VIII, Louis XII and François I. Chenonceau was begun in 1515 for Thomas Bohier, receiver-general of the finances for Normandy. Azay-le-Rideau (1518–27) was constructed by the financier Gilles Berthelot.

Women, as heiresses, wives, widows and mistresses, played an important role in the building of many châteaux. Anne Gedoyn, widow of Jean Le Breton, seigneur of Villesavin and Villandry, directed the works at Chambord from 1543 until her death in 1547. Chenonceau promotes itself as the *château des dames* —remodelled successively by Diane de Poitiers, Catherine de Medici and Louise of Savoy.

Henri IV's accession to the throne in 1589 prompted the reconstruction of two great châteaux. Charles II de Cossé of Brissac, was the Governor of Paris who opened the gates of the city to the new king in 1594. Twelve years later Brissac was created a duchy in his favour, and Charles embarked on an ambitious building scheme. The Château de Sully-sur-Loire was acquired in 1602 by Maximilien de Béthune, and was raised to a duchy for him in 1606, the same year as Brissac. The **Duc de Sully** was Grand Master of the Artillery and as Surintendant des Finances et des Bâtiments led the reconstruction of France after the Wars of Religion. After the assassination of Henri IV in 1610 he retired to Sully to cultivate his vast estates and write his famous memoirs.

During the reign of **Louis XIII** (1610–43) the grandest Loire château of the period was built by Cardinal Richelieu. The great Château de Richelieu

3

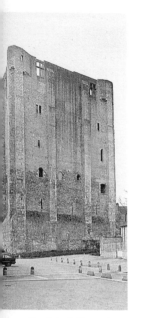

The late 11th-century *donjon* of Beaugency.

(which was grander than Vaux-le-Vicomte) was built to the designs of Jacques Le Mercier (also architect of Richelieu's palace in Paris, now the Palais-Royal). The château alas was demolished in 1805 for the value of its materials. Cheverny, built in the 1630s for Henri Hurault, governor and bailiff of Blois, happily survives. So does François Mansart's great wing at Blois, begun in 1635 for **Gaston d'Orléans,** brother of Louis XIII, who had been exiled to the Loire on account of his constant intriguing at court. The older part of Ménars, dating from 1637, was built for Guillaume Cuarron, Trésorier Général de L'Extraordinaire des Guerres. Antoine, Earl Walsh, who bought and extended Serrant, was an Irish shipowner, established at Nantes. The delightful Montgeoffroy was rebuilt in the early 1770s for the Maréchal de Contades. Legendre de Villemorien, who began remodelling Valençay in 1767, was a *fermier-général* (tax-gatherer).

Until recently the history of the Loire châteaux stopped effectively at 1800, but attention has recently focused on the amazing series of late 19th-century houses in the Sologne, south of Orléans. Here, following the arrival of the railway, **Napoleon III** handed out vast parcels of land to newly enriched industrialists and financiers. In the Sologne more than 340 châteaux were built between 1800 and 1914, and nearly half of these date from the years 1890–1914. A remarkable number survive, only a few as yet chronicled. They are often to be found at the end of long drives. Few are visible from the road and there are rarely gate-piers to announce them. So if you decide to explore be prepared to arrive in front of a modern bungalow.

The architecture

The earliest survivals are the *donjons*, the equivalent of the keeps of Norman castles in England. These were almost always strategically sited and no one knew better the value of a good site than Fulk Nerra. From 987, when he succeeded his father as Count of

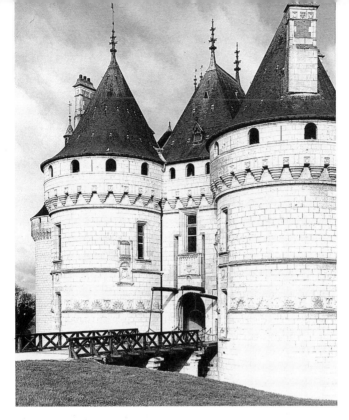

Anjou, until his death in 1040, his life was devoted to fighting and in particular to encircling the city of Tours and cutting in two the lands of his chief rivals, the Counts of Blois. Whenever he conquered a piece of land he built a fortress. The keep at Langeais, for example, threatens Tours from the west, and stands at the crest of a long spur between the Loire and Roumer rivers. The first *donjons* would have been built of wood but these have all disappeared or been rebuilt in stone. In plan they were square or rectangular with flat buttresses at the corners and consisted internally of one large chamber on each floor. The tall stone *donjon* at Beaugency, dating from the end of the 11th century, is specially impressive though it is hemmed in by later buildings and can no longer be visited. The near contemporary *donjon* at Loches was built for Fulk Nerra.

Pride of place among the **medieval fortresses** of the Loire goes to Angers, a vast enceinte, or walled enclosure, with 16 massive towers, built at the orders of Saint-Louis (Louis IX) in just ten years between 1230 and 1240, and as massive and impregnable looking as a great crusader castle in the Holy Land. Loches, and the more ruinous Chinon, are both major military defences, which evolved with outworks and encircling walls.

Many châteaux, even as late as the 17th century, were built with drawbridges. Even if these have vanished, the evidence has often survived in the form of a recess in the stonework for both bridge and chains, or levers, to fold back into. Typically there would have been two drawbridges, one for riders and another for those on foot. Inside the entrance arch look out for the portcullis or the vertical channel in which it was once set. In the vault there will sometimes be murder holes, not for pouring boiling oil through, but for ramming rods down on the attackers.

The devastation of the Hundred Years War left all too little record of the century between 1350 and 1450, but in the later 15th century the **moated castle** on a regular quadrangular plan became the dominant form. Le Plessis-Bourré (1468–73) and Le Moulin (c. 1480–1500) are two specially beautiful examples. Both sit in square moats with a gatehouse approached across a bridge. At this date, there are usually few windows of any size in the outside walls, but for all the wealth of defensive detail—drawbridges, machicolations, battlements, gunloops—15th-century château architecture, like that of most contemporary castles in England, was intended as much for chivalrous show as for serious defence.

The views of châteaux in one of the most famous of all late-medieval illuminated manuscripts, *Les Très Riches Heures du Duc de Berry*, show a series of castles with fairy-tale silhouettes of pointed towers, gilded weather vanes and ornate roof cresting. The form of Saumur today is much as it is shown in *Les Très Riches Heures*, even if the skyline has lost much of its exuberance.

The towers on most French *châteaux forts* have

(Opposite) Saumur as recorded in the 14th-century manuscript of *Les Très Riches Heures du Duc de Berry*. This shows the original exuberance of the ornamental detail concentrated in the silhouette.

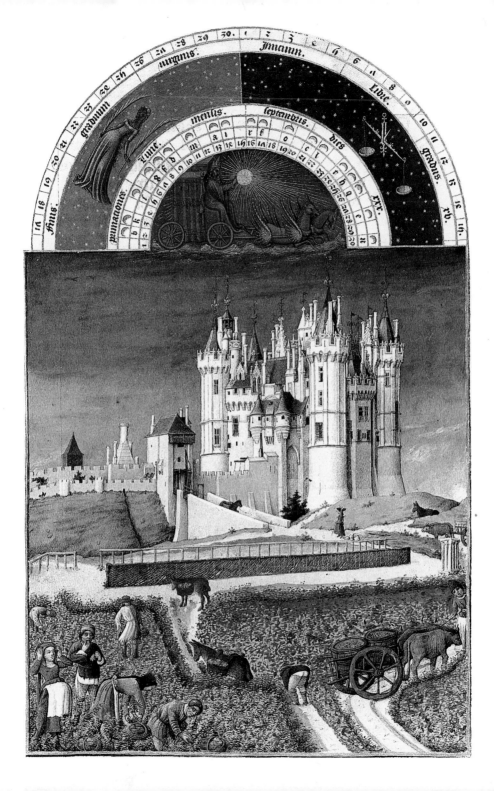

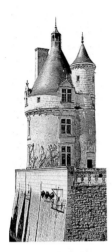

Chenonceau: the
15th-century *donjon*
was preserved
beside the
Renaissance
château.

machicolations (corbelled crenellations), which often
support wall-walks (*chemins-de-ronde*). These wall-
walks are almost always covered (in contrast to the
battlements of English castles) and may continue
along the walls between the towers. In many cases the
floor of the wall-walk consists simply of planks and
gives a precipitous view of the moat below. This was
intentional as it enabled defenders to rain missiles
down on anyone approaching or scaling the walls. The
towers of most *châteaux forts* are round (usually with
conical roofs), rather than square, as missiles glanced
off a curved surface. From the wall-walk it is usually
possible to see how the towers were placed to protect
each stretch of wall.

In many châteaux an earlier *donjon*, usually taller or
larger than the other towers, is retained, even at the
expense of upsetting the symmetry of plan or elevation. Examples are Ussé, Azay-le-Rideau and Chenonceau. Elsewhere, the circular towers, at the front
of the enceinte, known usually as *poivrières*, or
pepperpot towers, are retained. These can be seen at
Le Lude and Brissac.

Towers were not only preserved, but incorporated
into new designs (Chambord was actually designed in
or shortly before 1519 with large medieval-looking
circular towers) because, for the French, towers,
particularly ancient ones, proclaimed rank and ancestry. As late as 1770 the Bailli de Mirabeau wrote:

> I have always felt, on seeing a château with towers at its
> corners, a sort of respect for the owner, unknown though
> he be; a fine house, deprived of these ornaments, has
> never seemed to me to be more than the dwelling place of
> a wealthy *bourgeois*.

The preservation of towers was but one aspect of the
continuity between **Gothic** and **Renaissance**. The steep
roofs, the tall dormers, the vertically linked windows
all survived; only the ornamental detail changed.
Many 16th-century châteaux retain rich **Flamboyant
Gothic** detail which tends to be concentrated on the
roof-line. Characteristic elements are richly pierced

balustrades of pointed arches or scrollwork, extravagant dormers, emphasized by diamond-shaped pinnacles at the sides and centres (the most elaborate examples incorporate little flying buttresses), and a forest of decorative leadwork on the roof—finials, weather vanes, and embossed and crested roof ridges. This elaborate leadwork was often renewed or re-introduced in the later 19th century.

Charles VIII brought back 22 Italian craftsmen to Amboise after the sack of Fornova in 1496, but little survives of their work, and classical vocabulary and Renaissance ornament only enter French architecture from about 1510 onwards. Among the new elements are pilasters that flank the windows—usually inset with panels of decorative carving—tapering or shell-headed pediments to the windows and machicolations inset with *coquilles*.

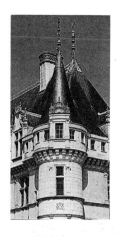

Azay-le-Rideau: turret with dormer window and decorative finial.

As in Italy, the classical orders, when first used, tended to be treated in a fairly free manner. Instead of following the proportions and detail of Doric, Ionic, or Corinthian, early Renaissance capitals tend to be squat, with the detail apparently left to the original carver rather as in the Romanesque style. Early Renaissance pilasters (columns and half-columns came a little later) are often rather short.

At the early Renaissance châteaux of Bury, Chenonceau and Azay-le-Rideau, emerges the distinct rhythm of windows alternating with large sections of plain wall, and string courses linking the panels beneath the windows. Compared with this light surface-patterning, François I's work at Blois and Chambord brought a new monumentality to French architecture. The designers were beginning to think in three dimensions. The famous octagonal staircase in the courtyard at Blois is massively modelled with arches set deep behind the pilasters. The upper cornice is of prodigious proportions and profile compared to that at Azay of only a few years earlier, and the top stage of the staircase tower carries a full entablature—architrave, richly carved frieze, and a cornice carved with a form of machicolations. These

Champigny-sur-
Veude: classical
doorway to the
chapel.

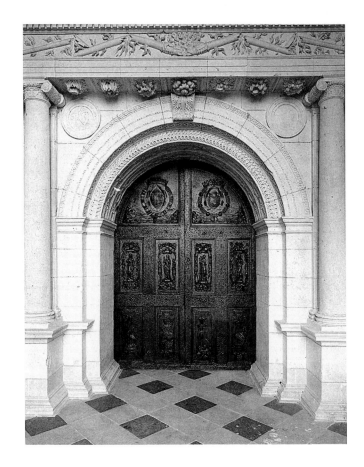

last also appear on the chimneystacks which are
adorned with pilasters and are as memorable as
miniature temples.

The names of individual architects or master masons
involved in pioneering the Renaissance in France are
slowly emerging. The greatest revelation is the probable extent of Leonardo da Vinci's role in the design
of Chambord. François I, and therefore no doubt
some of his courtiers also, evidently had the same
working knowledge of classical architecture as the
leading Italian noblemen. French masons took to the
new vocabulary with astonishing youthful vigour. The
carving on the exterior of the staircase at Azay-le-

Rideau, for example, is of quite sensational quality and delicacy.

Symmetry in plan, if not in elevation, was already well established in the 15th century; the Renaissance brought a new emphasis on that favourite French phenomenon, the axis. At Bury, for example, the main axis runs unbroken from the entrance, through the *corps-de-logis*, to the chapel on the far side of the garden.

From the 1540s a plain, more correct, classical style emerges without the riot of decorative carving. A good example is Champigny-sur-Veude. Here in the entrance to the chapel are textbook examples of correct Roman, Ionic and Corinthian columns and correctly proportioned arches and niches. The decorative carving is concentrated on the entablature and the columns stand on pedestals that Palladio might have drawn.

The **17th century** saw brick in fashion; the characteristic Henri IV or Louis XIII château is of red brick with stone dressings to the windows and quoins at the corners. Good examples are Brissac, the garden front of Cheverny, and La Morinière. One of the delights of early 17th-century châteaux is the formality of the approach, with an *avant-cour* flanked by matching blocks of *communs* on either side and pairs of pavilions or gate lodges. The geometrical perfection is often emphasized by a moat, as at La Ferté-Saint-Aubin, or a dry moat, as at La Ferté-Imbault.

The most accomplished work of this date is François Mansart's Orléans wing at Blois, the *corps-de-logis* of a huge quadrangular palace that was intended to cover the entire site. Here emerges the superbly sophisticated treatment of the orders that was to be the hallmark of French architecture for more than a century, with pilasters, half-columns and columns used to build up climaxes and create rhythms.

Architecturally there is relatively little to represent Louis XIV or Louis XV in the Loire, but the **neo-classicism** associated with Louis XVI (1774–89) appears with impressive vigour in the courtyard of

Valençay, and with an elegant restraint at Montgeof-froy. Neo-classicism brought a new discipline, and ornament is based on the classical orders or is faithfully naturalistic.

The countryside south of Orléans is an excellent hunting ground for large, opulent, **19th-century houses** built in a variety of styles. Bonhôtel (1875–82) represents the thoroughgoing but spirited contemporary Loire revival found in American châteaux such as Biltmore in North Carolina. Vouzeron, by the architect of Waddesdon Manor, Buckinghamshire, is a virtuoso essay in Flamboyant Gothic revival. South of Gien, Pont-Chevron has the immaculate *beaux-arts* assurance of the RAC club in London's Pall Mall.

Interiors

Centuries of neglect and 19th-century restoration, often of a thoroughgoing and cavalier kind, has left all too little trace of medieval interiors, except chimneypieces, staircases and occasional vaults.

The large spiral staircases of the 15th century are particularly impressive, culminating in the great circular ramps at Amboise, wide enough for horses and litters or carriages. Look out for those late medieval examples where the central newel post becomes a twisting handrail, leaving a void about the size of an old penny running right down the centre. The Gothic form was continued in the remarkable octagonal Renaissance staircases at Blois and Chambord, as well as at Montsoreau. At Azay-le-Rideau and Serrant, and later at Cheverny, is the Italian form with a single flight enclosed between solid walls, and doubling back on itself.

A hint of Renaissance richness survives at Blois in two richly carved stone doorcases. There is also an exquisite *cabinet*, or study, with four tiers of carved and gilt decorative panels. Hidden cupboards are opened by levers concealed behind the skirting.

Internally, the huge Renaissance palace of Chambord, with its central staircase and Greek Cross plan, is pure architecture; the four corners, however, are arranged into pairs of apartments—the second being in the large circular towers. At Le Lude fine wall paintings survive dating from the second half of the 16th century. The largest cycle of 16th-century murals —comparable with those at Fontainebleau—is to be found in the great first-floor gallery at Oiron, portraying scenes from the Trojan Wars.

Seventeenth-century interiors are well represented. Brissac survives in its original state. The scale is stupendous, with huge walls cloaked in vast tapestries. Here are some of the richest open-beamed ceilings *à la française* to be found anywhere, in parts carved, as well as painted and gilded with casket-like landscape scenes alternating with cartouches and grotesques.

Brissac: the early 17th-century Salle des Gardes with characteristic open-beam ceiling.

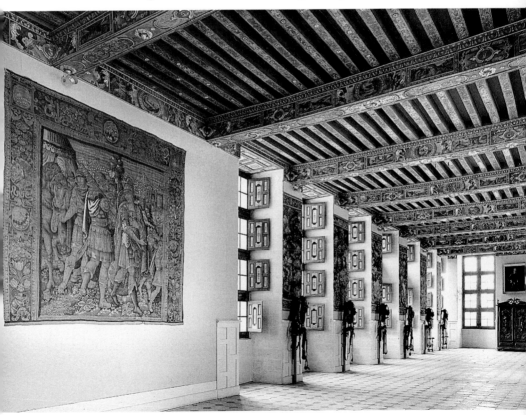

The shutters of the main room are painted to match, front and back, so the decoration is visible whether they are closed or open.

At Cheverny the early 17th-century carving and plasterwork is still more voluptuous, with panelled dados beneath the tapestries, painted with emblematic scenes, while the coffered ceilings contain both painted and sculpted ornament. Beauregard contains one of the largest examples of a baroque portrait gallery commissioned (in 1676) as a single decorative scheme with 325 historical portraits.

Montgeoffroy is a remarkable 18th-century example because it retains intact the greater part of its original furniture which can be checked against an inventory taken when the remodelling was completed in 1773. All the pearl-grey Louis-Seize *boiseries* survive as well as the original hangings in the bedrooms.

At Serrant, Napoleon's bedchamber contains fine Empire furniture and there are also a number of delightful contemporary wallpapers and borders. At Valençay the Chambre de Ferdinand VII contains a set of *grisaille* wallpaper scenes of 1814–15 by Dufour, portraying the life of Psyche.

A highly successful 19th-century restoration is the François I wing at Blois. Here there are a rich series of restored rooms by Duban, with painted and gilt decoration painted on canvas or directly on the walls. Elsewhere the best pieces of 19th-century work tend to be the huge carved stone chimneypieces; there is one at Chaumont with three openings which you can virtually walk into.

A sympathetic restoration, more in an arts and crafts vein, was carried out at the Château du Moulin towards 1900, with tiled floors and stencilled wall decoration.

Layout

The size and layout of a medieval castle depended on the extent of the household. In the later Middle Ages quite minor nobles had their own retainers and in times of unrest professional soldiers were regularly hired by leading noblemen. This led to a gradual separation of the household. The *donjon* had originally been the focus, but now it often became a more private place where the lord would retreat with his family. Security was important, but comfort too became a consideration: larger windows appeared and fireplaces proliferated. The first 'state' apartments often consisted of anti-chamber, council chamber, bedchamber and *garderobe.*

Staircases formed a major feature of French châteaux from the Renaissance onwards. There is an interesting contrast here with Palladio, who tended, in his country villas, to set staircases to the side, out of sight, as they disturbed the symmetry of the plan. At Azay, Cheverny and Serrant the Renaissance staircase is the dominating feature of the whole internal layout, set immediately behind the central front door and taking the place of a grand entrance hall. These first Renaissance staircases are very architectually treated and constructed in the same masonry as the exterior— though the carved detail, protected as it is from the elements, has usually survived much better. At Azay the staircase actually looks out through open arches directly into the courtyard.

A vivid picture of the layout of French châteaux is provided in a letter from Lady Holland to her sister in 1765:

> I dined and supp'd very frequently at their villas so that I am *au fait* of their way of life in the country. Their houses are in general excellent; no people have ever studied so much or succeeded so well in enjoying all the conveniences of life as the French do. There is always a large *salon*, an antechamber and eating-room together. Then above stairs you always have a long gallery, out of which you go into various apartments, some for single people, some for *mari et femme*

In French houses, then as now, much more emphasis was placed on formal conversation. Rarely do you see large comfortable armchairs and sofas as you would find in England or America, in which you can relax and read or sleep. The chairs are more upright—to concentrate the mind as well as improve the posture, and arranged, or stand ready to be arranged, in a large circle so everyone can participate in the same conversation. Eighteenth-century inventories list quite remarkable numbers of chairs in the principal rooms. At Montgeoffroy, for example, in the *salon* there were 18 *fauteuils* and *chaises en cabriolet* (with curved backs), two *canapés* (sofas) and eight matching *fauteuils à la Reine* (with flat backs), four *fauteuils* with square backs, and four *bergères* (large, deep armchairs filled in beneath the arms), most of which are still in the room. Some rooms must have looked extraordinarily cramped as a remark in Blondel's *Cours d'Architecture* (1771–77) confirms:

> There are some architects who, in the decoration of apartments, make a habit of repeating false doors either in symmetry or opposition to the real ones, with the result that in a room where many chairs are essential some must be placed in front of the false doors, which does not give a very natural appearance.

Dining-rooms tend not to appear in French châteaux until the later 18th century. The more normal practice was to eat off movable tressles or occasional tables in whichever room the family was sitting. The habit, by this time fairly widespread in England and America, of sitting down at a single large table, sometimes for as long as four or five hours, was virtually unknown. The young Duc de Rochefoucauld, who first experienced it in Suffolk, found it 'one of the most wearisome of English experiences'.

The French were very keen games players and in almost every *salon* there will be one or more *trictrac* (backgammon) tables. In some houses an *antichambre* is in effect a games room. Many houses also contain fine libraries, with bookcases designed as part of the architecture. One of the grandest is on the first floor at Serrant. Furnished as a huge family room it has up to 16 shelves of books with a continuous rod along which a ladder is moved to reach the highest shelves.

A standard feature of houses at least until the mid-17th century was a Salles des Gardes—serving as a retainers' hall or armoury. This is almost always one of the largest rooms in the château, with a magnificent fireplace, a counterpart of the great hall in English houses. The early 17th-century Salle des Gardes at Brissac, however, is on the first floor and much more akin to an Elizabethan long gallery.

The main *appartement* consisting of bedchamber, and sometimes an antechamber as well, is usually on the ground floor. This is the arrangement at Montgeoffroy. Here the *appartement* of the Maréchal de Contades consists of a small study and splendid bedroom beyond. The bed is set with great *éclat* in a very tall alcove crowned with military trophies. On the other side of the central *salon*, on the garden front, is the Appartement de Madame Herrault, the companion of the Maréchal in the closing years of his life.

While the Maréchal and his mistress slept on the ground floor, the first floor was occupied entirely by bedrooms for family and guests. Lady Holland describes the typical arrangement in a French château. Those for *mari et femme* consist:

of a little antechamber which communicates to two bedchambers, a room for each servant, and a *garderobe*

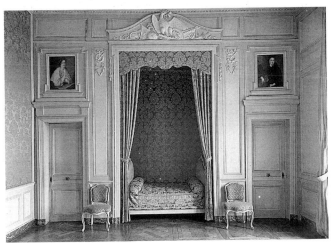

Montgeoffroy: the restrained Louis-Seize decoration in the bedroom of the Maréchal de Contades.

for each bedchamber, sometimes a *cabinet de toilette* for madame.

Those for single people were composed 'of a bedchamber, servant's room, and *garderobe*, and sometimes a closet besides'. La Rochefoucauld contrasts the typical country house in England at the time:

> The English do not trouble at all about the pleasure of making a really satisfactory arrangement of rooms. In an English house you never see a private door, a private room, or a closet.

One of the places where you have a rare, perhaps even unique, opportunity to study the domestic arrangements of a Loire château is at La Ferté-Saint-Aubin, where you are free to walk round the entire house, and inspect the cellars and attics, and work out where all the little doors opening in and out of French 18th-century bedrooms actually lead.

Virtually every room in a 17th- or 18th-century château had its own fireplace and if these were kept lit, the whole house would remain very warm. Châteaux-owners, like country-house owners in England and America, were often keen to introduce the latest technology and conveniences into their houses. At Serrant there is a complete system of underfloor heating, dating apparently from about 1850 and still in use. The floor vents have particularly fine brass grilles. Also at Serrant is a delightful example of a hand-operated lift of about 1900, rising in the well of a handsome staircase of this date.

The court

Inspired by Joan of Arc, liberation from English rule began in the Loire Valley. Under Charles VII the court was often in the Loire and Amboise became the residence of the dauphin, the future Louis XI. Later Charles VIII brought Italian artists and craftsmen there, and Louis XII made Blois a virtual second capital. But thanks largely to the researches of Robert Knecht, the fullest picture we have of court life is in the reign of François I, who from the beginning declared he would create a court to rival those of Italy and form the setting for the absolute monarch of united France.

Under François I the court grew considerably in size and importance. As inflation bit into landed revenues in the early 16th century, the nobility looked to court for offices, pensions and other royal favours, a process which in turn helped increase the King's authority, or absolutism.

By 1523 the king's household (*hôtel du roi*) comprised 540 officials, more than twice the number on the payroll of Louis XI's household in 1480. These included chaplains, doctors, barbers, gentlemen of the chamber, valets, cupbearers, carvers, grooms, pages, secretaries, quartermasters, porters, musicians, spit-turners, sauce-makers, pastry-cooks and tapestry-makers. The court included four further departments: the *argenterie*, which purchased clothes and furniture, the *écurie* which looked after the horses and employed numerous messengers and the *venneries* and *fauconneries* which organized the royal hunts. The queen, the queen mother and the royal children all had separate households.

At Amboise or Blois, as elsewhere, the King's day began with a *levée* in the presence of leading courtiers and important guests. This was followed by a council meeting. After mass at 10 a.m. came lunch. Afterwards the King received ambassadors or deputations.

The afternoon was usually free for hunting or outdoor pursuits. In the evening François would dine with his family, followed regularly by a ball or a masque. The king used to say it was necessary to give a ball twice a week to live at peace with his subjects.

For much of the year the court was constantly on the move. 'Never during the whole of my embassy', wrote one Venetian ambassador on a mission of some months, 'was the court in the same place for more than fifteen consecutive days.'

According to the Italian sculptor Benvenuto Cellini 12,000 horses were used to transport the court. The

Blois: the salamander
of François I adorns
an overmantle.

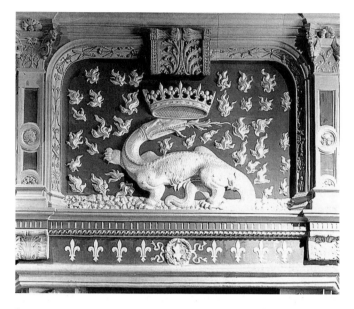

baggage train included furniture, gold and silver plate
and tapestries. Only a few of the most frequented
royal châteaux were kept furnished; the others remained empty between visits.

Jousts and mock battles were a favourite court
entertainment. At Amboise in April 1518, the King
led 600 men on an attack of a model town complete
with a moat and gun battery defended by the Dukes of
Bourbon and Vendôme. 'It was the finest battle ever
seen', wrote Florange, 'and the nearest to real war-
fare, but the entertainment did not please everyone
for some were killed—and others terrified.'

While Louis XII favoured falconry, François I
preferred to ride to hounds. A treatise of 1561 calls
him the *'père des veneurs'*. François I increased the
number of huntsmen who hunted with greyhounds,
white dogs and trapping nets in the way so often shown
in tapestries.

The King's courage, in the hunt as on the battlefield,
was legendary. The story was told that during celebra-
tions at Amboise in 1515 he was only prevented from
fighting a wild boar by entreaties from the queen and

his mother. The boar instead was left to batter dummies in the courtyard of the château, but then forced its way up a staircase. Here the king faced the beast and ran it through with his sword remaining as calm 'as if he had seen a damsel coming towards him'.

After the defeat of François I at Pavia, Spain, in 1525, the court moved to the Ile de France and Paris became the centre of the kingdom. Building work was concentrated on châteaux around Paris; in an architectural sense this was a blessing as the Renaissance work in the Loire largely escaped remodelling.

Gardens

While late medieval Loire castles undoubtedly had gardens, and extensive castle gardens are portrayed in illuminated manuscripts, it is as yet difficult to relate specific views to surviving castle precints. The appeal of a garden in the Middle Ages, as described in the medieval tale of courtly love, the *Roman de la Rose*, was to the senses, particularly those of smell and hearing; many scented flowers and herbs were grown and caged singing birds were kept.

The Renaissance brought conscious formality of design with an emphasis on exact measurements, symmetry and proportion. A French Renaissance garden was, as a result, very architectural and planned as an integral part of the layout of a château. Bury, west of Blois, begun in 1511, was important in making the garden the climax of the main axis through the house.

All too little, alas, survives of the enormous Renaissance gardens shown in the beautiful bird's-eye views drawn by the architect and engraver, **Jacques Androuet du Cerceau.** (His two volumes, *Les plus excellents bâtiments de France*, 1576 and 1579, are the main source of visual information about 16th-century French garden design.) However, Charles VIII's terrace at Amboise, towering above the river, is there waiting to be restored. Charles's interest in gardens is revealed in a letter he wrote to the Cardinal de

Bourbon after his arrival in Naples. 'You would not credit the fine gardens I have seen in this town.' The garden at Amboise was divided into ten squares each surrounded by rails. The main feature was a large wooden pavilion sheltering a fountain.

Rather more is known of the great garden at Blois. Dom Antonio de Beatis, describing the Cardinal of Aragon's visit in 1517, wrote:

> All these gardens are the work of Don Pacello, the Neapolitan priest who is very expert in such matters and was brought to France by Charles on his return from Naples.

Pacello's contribution is likely nonetheless to have been the planting more than the design. The garden at Blois was divided into ten compartments. Beatis wrote, 'the big garden is entirely surrounded by galleries wide and long so that horses can go there.' He saw 'many lemon and orange trees in wooden tubs. In the winter they are kept in a big wooden shelter which protects them from snow.' (Glasshouses were only introduced in the 18th century when glass manufacture improved.) Beatis continues, 'there are also many plants and herbs for salad, endives and cabbages as fine as those in Rome.'

The most important 16th-century treatise is *L'Agriculture et Maison Rustique* (1564) by Charles Estienne and Jean Liébault which provides details of the type of plant that was grown at this time. For hedges they recommend hazel, currant bushes, raspberry canes, pepper plants, brambles, honeysuckle, viburnum, holly, wild apple and privet. Both the *parterre* and the *potager* are surrounded by covered walks made of trellis, to support climbing plants like jasmine, musk rose, ivy, cucumber, tomatoes and peas. The *parterre*, wrote Liébault, should be in two parts, one for flowers for cutting, the other for plants grown mainly for their scent. In the first group he mentions violets, marigolds, pinks, pansies, daisies and wallflowers; in the second, numerous herbs.

The word *parterre* was used to describe the flower garden as a whole—the compartments are called

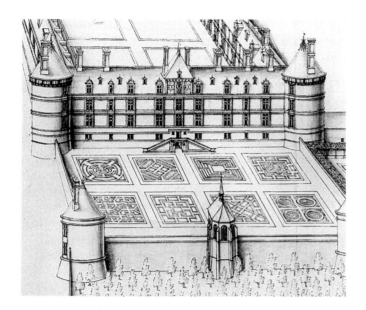

Bury: detail of du Cerceau engraving showing the formal *parterre* with a different pattern in each compartment.

entrelacs (knots), or *carreaux* (squares, or literally tiles). The design of each compartment was complete in itself and each one was a different geometric pattern from its neighbours—squares, circles, diamonds and crosses predominated as motifs—often forming miniature labyrinths. In baroque gardens four compartments might together form a single overall pattern, rather as four different Portuguese tiles are often needed today to make a repeating pattern.

Seventeenth-century formality is represented by the great garden terrace overlooking the Loir at Le Lude, and the vestiges of the large park and plantations of Sully-sur-Loire. At Ménars, the spectacular formal terraces overlooking the Loire survive, dating from Soufflot's work at the château which included a neo-classical rotunda and orangeries. The best example of a 19th-century park in the English style is at Chaumont, while the return to formal gardening around 1900 is beautifully represented by Pont-Chevron's clipped hedges, pleached *allées* and arbours.

The recreation of a Renaissance garden at Villandry

at the beginning of this century was on a scale unrivalled until the great restoration carried out at Het Loo in Holland in the early 1980s. Now another garden has been recreated on an ambitious scale at the Château de Chamerolles, north-east of Orléans.

Landscapes and forests

Perceptions of beauty in landscape vary strongly from one century, even one generation, to another. For the Romantic Movement, fine scenery meant mountains —the Scottish Highlands or the Alps. In the 16th and 17th centuries untamed nature had little such appeal, and the Loire valley delighted travellers precisely because it was so intensely and neatly cultivated. 'It might be called the Arcadia of France', Cardinal Bentivoglio wrote in 1619. To the Maréchal de Vielleville the delight of the journey from Paris to Nantes was to find it, 'just one suburb'.

There has always been a focus on the river itself. The Loire is broad and often sluggish and on a dull day, particularly after too rich a dinner the night before, you may find yourself agreeing with Victor Hugo: 'a broad and yellow river, flat banks, poplars everywhere'. But on a clear, bright, balmy morning, few could agree with Hugo's jaundiced view. On either side of Tours, where the road on both banks borders the river, the views are breathtaking—a panorama as exhilarating, if not as dramatic, as the Rhine north of Koblenz.

The special beauty of châteaux like Chaumont and Ussé, Amboise and Saumur, is their perfect relation with the villages and towns below them. The lines of houses along the river, with a wooded bank above and often a grass verge below, are an enchanting sight, their very modesty providing the perfect counterpoint to the majestic castles on the rock above. The small towns and villages, still very much alive, are always enjoyable to explore.

Hunting was the most popular pastime and the forests around many châteaux remain very extensive.

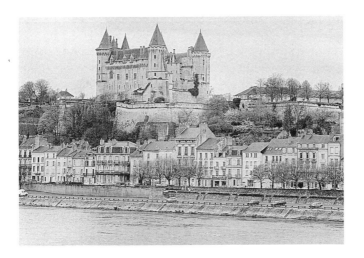

Saumur towers
above a picturesque
row of old houses
along the bank of the
Loire.

Usually these were cut through with a grid of long straight rides, occasionally bisected by diagonals to form star-shaped plantations. These can easily be spotted on the Michelin map—most obviously around Blois. To the west of the town is the forest of Blois, to the south the forest of Russy, to the east that of Chambord. It is worth making a small detour on one of these forest roads to sense the size of the royal hunting reserves.

The classic medieval treatise on hunting, *Le Livre de la Chasse* of Gaston Phoebus, describes hunting with spears, javelins, three-pronged swords, long-bows, crossbows, hunting swords and hunting knives. In France as in much of Europe wild boar, even more than stags, were the prize prey. Following the growing use of guns in the 15th and 16th centuries shooting became more popular.

While the great forest around Chambord soon becomes monotonous the Sologne countryside south of Orléans is more varied and gloriously unspoilt, with vast, well-maintained sporting estates, alternating with attractive red-brick villages. Here, long straight roads are virtually empty of traffic, pheasants strut along the verges, and meadows alternate with large deciduous woods.

25

Restoration

The Revolution was responsible for surprisingly little in the way of direct destruction, but in succeeding years many châteaux suffered from total neglect and pilfering. The Château de Richelieu was sold by Napoleon to a demolition contractor and in 1823 Chanteloup met the same fate. Blois, curiously, owes its survival to the Revolution: Louis XVI had decreed its sale and demolition in 1788, but the order was never carried out. But by 1828 Balzac found it in a state of degradation that was a national disgrace. Twelve years later the Commission des Monuments Historiques was established and the restoration first of Blois, then of Chambord began.

The French invented the Magic Kingdom a century before Disney—or so one might conclude from the major restorations carried out at many of the great Loire châteaux in the 19th century. In some cases these restorations were fanciful to the point of being cavalier. In the courtyard at Chaumont, the architect took away the Flamboyant balconies beneath the first-floor windows and replaced them by a balcony on the second, for no other apparent reason than to heighten the romantic effect.

What interests me is the role photography may have played in perceptions of the Loire châteaux. For photographs capture reflection in a way that paintings or prints never can. And much of the romantic beauty of the Loire châteaux comes from their association with water—towering above the river or set langorously in moats—or, as with Chenonceau, actually built out across the river.

At Azay-le-Rideau the moat on the east side was enlarged in the 1870s, specifically to create a better reflection. The creator of Villandry's superb formal gardens, Joachim Carvallo, explained in an article in 1924 how he had decided to demolish the 18th-century terrace around the château, so that the walls descended sheer into the water, ' ...and as the water constitutes a mirror, the château reflects itself, repro-

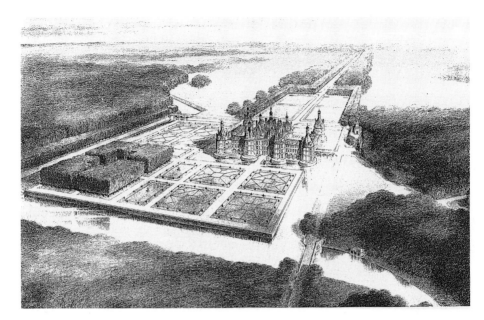

ducing the image of its architecture.'

Chambord is often photographed with its sensational silhouette reflected in a moat, yet when you are there, there is no sign of water beneath the walls. It is, in fact, on the far side of the gardens—encircling the *parterre* not the château. Few visitors make the trek to the far end of the gardens, yet here is a favoured spot for photographers.

Once again, the waters of Chambord prove to be a product of early 20th-century romanticism. True, du Cerceau showed the château encircled by moats, but these were not excavated. It fell to the landscape architect **Achille Duchêne** (1866–1947) to imagine what Chambord and its gardens would look like surrounded by broad moats; but in the event it was only the river at the far end of the *parterre* that was straightened to look like a canal.

In the Sologne, 19th-century owners sought old seigneurial sites for their new châteaux, but as there were not enough to go round, any ancient farm with a *bassecour*, or better still an old mill with the water essential for a large lake, were swept up.

View of Chambord by Achille Duchêne, 1910, showing Duchêne's proposed scheme for surrounding the château with moats.

27

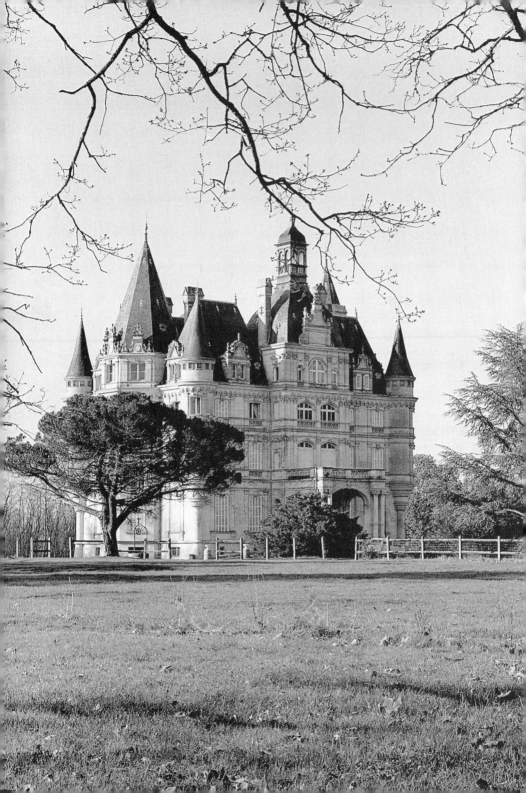

GAZETTEER OF THE CHATEAUX

Amboise should be one of the great royal châteaux of France—as sumptuous and extensive as Blois or even Fontainebleau. It reached its zenith under Charles VIII and François I who crowned the promontory above the town with courtyards and gardens to create a veritable Alhambra. This magnificent complex is recorded in two superb bird's-eye views of the 1570s by Jacques Androuet du Cerceau. But alas the tale of the château's destruction is almost as significant as that of its creation.

Since the Gallo-Roman period there were fortifications on the site, and in 1030 Fulk Nerra reconstructed a collegiate church, that had been founded in 1014, and dedicated it to Saint Florentin. This no longer survives, but is shown in the centre of du Cerceau's view. About 1115 the original château was built by Hugues d'Amboise. At the beginning of the 14th century the family divided into two branches, the elder retaining Amboise, the younger settling at Chaumont.

After Louis d'Amboise had been imprisoned for conspiracy against Charles VII's favourite Georges de la Trémoille, Amboise became royal property. Louis XI modernized the ancient fortress, but withdrew to the château of Plessis-lès-Tours, installing Queen Charlotte of Savoy and her children here. The future Charles VIII was born and brought up at Amboise which became his favoured residence. A huge building programme was launched in 1491, which the Florentine ambassador likened to the laying out of a town. The accounts provide the names of the masons in charge: Colin Biart, Guillaume Senault, Louis Armangeart, and their collaborators, Martin and Bastien François, Pierre Trinqueau and Jacques Sourdeau—names that recur in other great works of the era.

AMBOISE

(*Opposite*) Bonhôtel at Ligny-le Ribault, built 1875–82 to the designs of Louis Parent in Renaissance style.

29

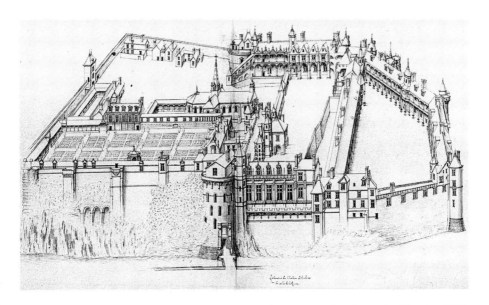

Amboise: 16th-century view by du Cerceau showing the royal château at its greatest extent.

Following his victorious campaign in Italy Charles VIII returned in 1496 with 22 Italian artists and writers in his train including the sculptor Guido Mazzoni, the architect Fra Giocondo, the carpenter and architect Domenico da Cortona (who made the model of Chambord) and Pacello di Mercogliano, *architecteur de jardins*, who all worked to transform Amboise into a luxurious palace. But two years later Charles was dead, having cracked his head on a doorway in the château. His successor, Louis XII d'Orléans, preferred Blois, but handed Amboise to Louise of Savoy, Charles' widow and mother of the future François I who ascended the throne in 1515. François I held a special affection for Amboise and completed a wing begun by Louis XII and installed Leonardo da Vinci nearby at Le Clos-Lucé (for Leonardo's work in France see the entry on Chambord).

Then decline set in. First came the Amboise conspiracy when Huguenots tried to seize the town and the king himself; when they failed more than 1,300 prisoners were hung from the balconies. In the 17th century Amboise became a royal prison, and in the 1760s was raised to a duchy for the Duc de Choiseul, who preferred to live at Chanteloup, where his remarkable pagoda survives.

30

Napoleon granted Amboise to Roger Ducos, a comrade from the era of the Consulat, who, to save on maintenance, razed the larger part of the château leaving only two wings (built by Charles VIII and François I) and the Chapelle Saint-Hubert.

At the Restoration Amboise was granted to the Duchesse d'Orléans, and was inherited by her son Louis-Philippe, the Citizen King. The Orléans family regained possession at the end of the century and the Duc d'Aumale entrusted the restoration of Amboise to the architects Victor and Gabriel Ruprich-Robert who largely reconstructed the interior. Following bombardment in 1940 the chapel was carefully restored by Bernard Vitry. Since 1974 the château has been in the hands of the Saint Louis Foundation.

Looking at the château from across the river you can see first of all the large cylinder of the Tour des Minimes shown by du Cerceau. To the right is the **Charles VIII Wing** with its tall mullioned windows and rich Gothic dormers; to the left is the great retaining wall of the once elaborate formal gardens. Peeping over the ramparts to the right of the Charles VIII wing, you should be able to see the slender spire of the Chapelle Saint-Hubert, shown projecting behind a galleried range at the top right of du Cerceau's view.

The approach today is up a ramp from the town, originally created as a means of access to the collegiate church but closed in the 15th century by Louis XI after the

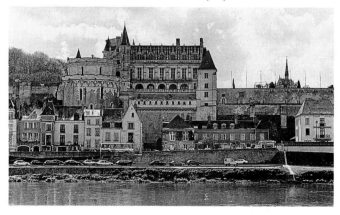

Amboise: the château seen from across the Loire with the town below.

31

construction of the parish church in the town. The ramp leads onto a terrace from where there is a wonderful view of the Loire and the surrounding countryside.

The tour begins with the exquisite Gothic **Chapelle Saint-Hubert** dating from 1491–8; the building is cruciform in plan with exceptionally rich lead cresting on the roof and a flèche (slender spire) adorned with antlers. There is a very fine relief over the portal by the sculptor Corneille de Nesve, portraying the legend of Saint Hubert (the patron saint of hunting) and the stag. Across the large courtyard, the Charles VIII wing with its Gothic detail, is clearly distinguishable from the wing completed under François I to the right, with dormers carrying clusters of characteristic huge Renaissance candelabra—most noticeable in the ogee dormers.

Inside there are a number of refurbished and redecorated rooms; the high point of the visit is the ascent of the upper part of the **Tour des Minimes**, built in 1495–6, by means of an extraordinary continuous circular ramp leading up from the town below, wide enough for a coach to ascend.

The best of the interiors is Ruprich-Robert's **Salle des États** in the Charles VIII wing, a neo-Gothic hall of particular elegance. It is given warmth and finesse by the red brick walls and beautifully crisp white stonework. The vaults are carried on what are, in effect, classically proportioned circular columns, despite their octagonal Gothic bases. The hooded fireplace, encrusted with fleurs-de-lis and ermines, is like a royal robe.

When you leave the enceinte be sure to make the descent by the **Tour Hurtault** (the entrance is through the shop) which takes you back into the town. Completed around 1500, this has the same continuous ramp as the Tour des Minimes, but is largely unrestored and retains a wealth of lively Gothic detail.

ANGERS

Angers is best seen at night, when it is floodlit and the walls of grey schist look black and are at their most overpowering. The brooding presence of the castle still completely dominates the town.

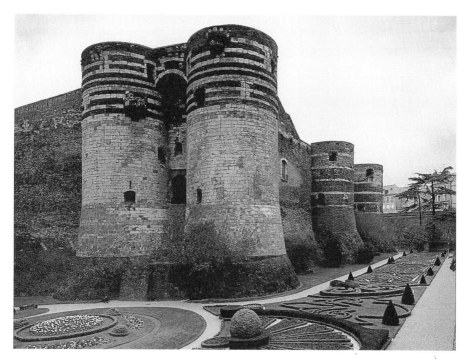

The château is surrounded by a broad, deep, dry moat; the complete enceinte, 660 m (720 yds) in length, is punctuated by 17 circular towers which originally would have had pointed roofs. What is hard to comprehend is that the whole complex, many times larger than any medieval cathedral, took just ten years to build from 1230 to 1240.

The 13th-century château at Angers and the newly laid out *parterres* in the moat.

Excavations in the castle have revealed the outline of the walls of a Gallo-Roman *oppidum*. From the ninth century the town became the seat of the Counts of Anjou, the most famous of whom, Fulk Nerra (987–1040), enlarged his lands by constant warring with his neighbours. His descendant Henry Plantaganet was crowned King of England in 1154, having two years earlier acquired by marriage the entire duchy of Aquitaine. Virtually nothing is known of Angers at this time. There is a record of a fire in 1132 destroying the great hall and collegiate church, while 20 years later an English visitor described the castle as a large building recently extended.

In 1203 King Philippe Auguste took Angers from King John of England; a new château was built by Saint Louis (Louis IX), who in 1246, gave Anjou to his brother Charles, later King of Naples.

In 1356 Anjou was granted by the King, Jean Le Bon, to his second son Louis, who in 1375, ordered the celebrated tapestry of *The Apocalypse* which now hangs in a modern exhibition hall inside the château. His son Louis II constructed the chapel in the courtyard at the beginning of the 15th century and the adjoining Logis Royal. Their son René, Duc de Lorraine by marriage, enlarged the residential buildings, planted gardens within the enceinte and even installed a menagerie. In 1471 he retired to Provence and ten years later Anjou was reabsorbed into the royal domain.

During the Wars of Religion in the 16th century the castle became a Catholic stronghold defying the Huguenots who, for short periods, seized the town. The architects Philibert de l'Orme and Jean de l'Étoile were involved in deepening the ditches and adding defensive outworks. Nonetheless the castle was taken by just 15 men in the course of a sudden Protestant assault in 1585 and Henri III gave orders that the walls and towers on the town side (not all of them, as is often said) should be pulled down.

The Governor was evidently reluctant to obey Henri's orders and by 1592 the six towers facing the town had lost no more than their pepperpot roofs. Subsequently all the towers were transformed into flat-topped gun batteries which you can see if you make the ascent of the walls.

Architecturally the most remarkable aspect of Angers is the sheer regularity in both plan and elevation achieved on so uneven a site. The towers are emphasized by bands of white limestone and granite. The builders evidently wished to make the castle look as if it grew from the natural rock—it is hard to tell, looking at the battered (sloping) bases of the towers, where the natural stone has been shaved away and where it has been built up to create such impressive regularity. The wall at the south end suffered the most from depredations though it provides a magnificent platform from which to view the river Maine.

However do not let Angers' mighty walls raise your expectations of what lies within. Much has been demolished and the **Logis Royal**, though it contains few very fine tapestries, is very plain. The ramparts, however, lead to a pleasant roof-top garden as well as providing vertiginous views of the recently planted *parterres* in the dry moats below.

For many Azay is the perfect Loire château, an enchanting blend of a fairy-tale Gothic silhouette and exquisite Renaissance detail and proportions—all on an intimate and positively covetable scale. Gothic are the steep roofs capped by slender lead finials, and the pepperpot turrets. Renaissance are the symmetry of the elevations, the expanses of plain wall and the windows framed by pilasters.

The fief is ancient, and is recorded in the tenth century; it passed into the royal domain under Philippe Auguste in 1223. In 1418 the château was devastated and the village

AZAY-LE-RIDEAU

Azay-le-Rideau (1518–27) reflected in the waters of the moat.

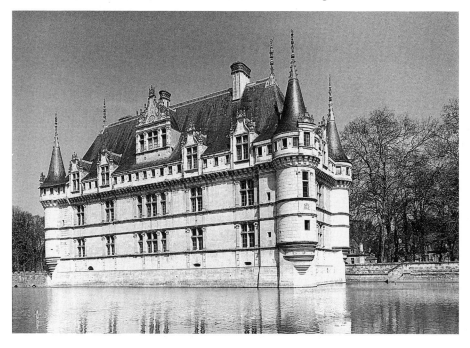

burnt—the name Azay-le-Brûlé appears in the 15th century. Towards the end of the century the *seigneurie* passed to a *maître de la chambre* of Louis XI and Charles VIII, Martin Berthelot. His son, Gilles, inherited in 1518 and immediately embarked on rebuilding. Gilles was a financier and entrusted the work to his wife Philippe, daughter and heiress of Antoine Lesbahy.

The surviving accounts provide the names of the masons, Denis Guillourt and Etienne Rousseau. The façades carry the initials of Gilles and his wife, and also the salamander of François I and the ermine of Queen Claude, who died in 1524, suggesting that the château was substantially complete by then. Three years later Berthelot was implicated in a financial scandal; he was seized and his property confiscated by the King (in just the same way the young Louis XIV was to seize Vaux-le-Vicomte and imprison its builder Nicolas Fouquet, his *surintendant des finances*, a century and a half later). François I gave Azay to Antoine Raffin his companion in arms at the battle of Pavia.

From 1787 the château was held by the four successive marquis de Biencourt; Antoine-Marie undertook a major restoration in 1845 with Dussillon as his architect and the work was continued after his death in 1854 by his son. Following his death Azay was acquired in 1905 by the state and is now run by the Caisse Nationale des Monuments Historiques.

The château built by Gilles Berthelot is in the form of an L, retaining a large medieval tower at the north-east corner (immediately to the right of the bridge). As at Chenonceau this was evidently done to emphasize seigneurial continuity. This tower shown in contemporary prints as being quite plain before 1850, was rebuilt with a pointed roof, pilasters and machicolations to match the rest of the château during the restoration by Dussillon. He also added the turret at the left corner of the *corps-de-logis* to match the one behind.

A considerable amount of the stonework was renewed in this period—notably many of the dormers, but the exquisite quality of the original carving can be seen on the arcaded front of the **Staircase**. This is positively Spanish in

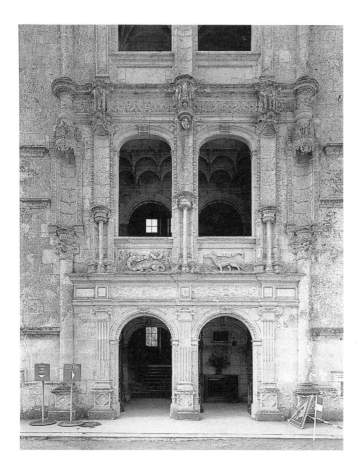

The early Renaissance carving on the entrance and staircase at Azay-le-Rideau.

its exuberance and the utterly unselfconscious mixture of Gothic and Renaissance detail. The ground floor has short fluted pilasters; the first floor, Gothic colonnettes and niches—though the detail is classical and almost as intricate as jewellery; on the second floor tall pilasters appear with the characteristic inset panels of the early Renaissance, still mixed with Gothic niches; on the top floor there are both tall and short pilasters, and a profusion of the candelabra and shells that were favourite motifs of the period. The salamander and ermine emblems appear over the doors, while the gable on the top is a classic example of the French Renaissance love of piling motif upon motif.

Detail showing François I's salamander over the entrance at Azay-le-Rideau.

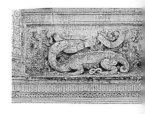

Azay-le-Rideau
1. Staircase

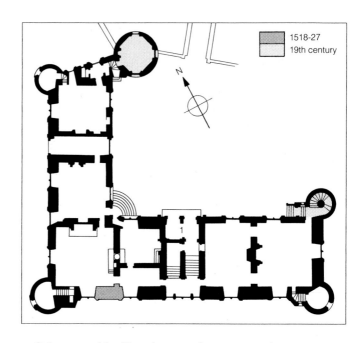

1518-27
19th century

Italianate carving on
a doorcase at Azay-
le-Rideau.

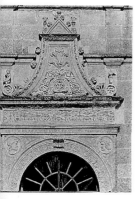

Other notable Renaissance features at Azay are two beautiful doorways set low on either side of the west wing linked by a vaulted corridor and the large ornate dormer windows that appear on all sides of the building.

It is essential to walk round to the south front and admire the exact symmetry of the **Façade** with a subtle central emphasis provided by the tiers of triple windows. Here, unlike the courtyard, there are both battlements and machicolations—though evidently of a purely ornamental nature.

Azay lies low, its site bathed by the waters of the Indre, and a major part of its beauty lies in the way the moat laps the castle walls, but this is a 19th-century innovation—or restoration—as a garden plan of about 1770 shows a walk beneath the walls with only the *avant-cour* being a true island. To the west the moat was enlarged still further to provide the reflections characteristic of the châteaux of the Loire. On the west front the (near) symmetry of the windows was only achieved with considerable juggling of the reveals as can be seen inside.

Such is the constant throng of visitors at Azay that the

rooms are very barely furnished, though attempts are being made to create a warmer, more lived-in, atmosphere. On the ground floor, note the original, lower level of the kitchen; in the main room beyond is a cast of a fireplace in the Château de Montal in Quercy: in the further room a splendid late 19th-century creation with an enormous salamander above the hearth. The **Grande Salle** on the first floor has ceiling beams of prodigious size and an early fireplace with finely sculpted capitals.

The joy of the interior is the **Staircase**. Here the superb stonework and vaulting has the quality of external architecture brought inside in its full richness. The traditional French staircase was a spiral, which became even larger during the 15th century and culminated in the great ramped towers at Amboise. At Azay the Italian form of straight enclosed flight returning dog-leg fashion was introduced almost for the first time. Here there are Gothic-type arches springing from corbels with pendant bosses, but in between are Renaissance portrait medallions.

BEAUGENCY

Beaugency is a formidable example of a tall and regular *donjon* or keep of the late 11th century. It was probably built for Raoul I *seigneur* of Beaugency from 1090 to 1130.

It is set back a little from the river and overlooks a small *place*. The interior, however, has been closed for some years as it is not considered safe for visitors. Raoul II, sold the *seigneurie* in 1291 to King Philippe le Bel and Charles V gave it to his son Louis Duc d'Orléans. The English took it in 1428, but it was liberated shortly after by Joan of Arc.

In 1441 Charles d'Orléans gave Beaugency to his half-brother, the Comte de Dunois, who built an elegant *logis* with a polygonal stair beside it. Inside, the accommodation consisted of a basement and four upper floors with very narrow windows. In 1308 the royal accounts mention the insertion of 18 windows in the staircase tower, which correspond approximately to the arched windows that can be seen today. The building now houses the local museum.

(Overleaf) View across the Loire to the late 11th-century *donjon* at Beaugency.

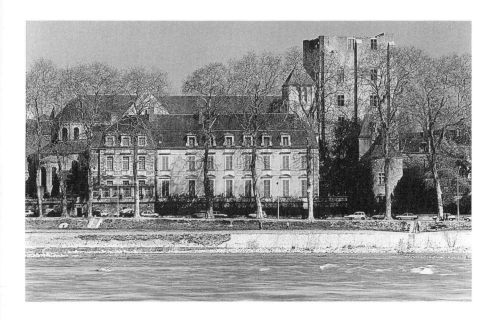

BEAUREGARD

Beauregard is approached along an axial avenue of positively ducal grandeur so it comes as a surprise to arrive at a modest *maison de plaisance* such as its name suggests.

In 1495 Louis d'Orléans, the future Louis XII, had made Beauregard a *seigneurie* in favour of Jean Doulcet. In 1521 François I granted the estate to his maternal uncle René of Savoy, whose widow lived on here after his death in 1525. In 1545 the château was sold to Jean du Thier, Seigneur of Ménars, one of Henri II's four secretaries of state, who died in 1559, the same year as his master; du Thier built the present château. The architecture of Beauregard is the cool, restrained classicism of the mid-16th century without the exuberance and solecisms of the early Renaissance.

Du Cerceau provides two views of the house, in one of which the present arcade is clearly visible. What has changed is that the building on the right, the Logis Doulcet, and an entrance tower have been demolished, in 1622 and 1810 respectively.

Du Thier is said to have commissioned Scibec de Carpi, an Italian artist working in Fontainebleau and the Louvre, to make the elaborate woodwork of the **Cabinet des Grelots** on the first floor. While the hexagonal ceiling could be of this date, the *boiseries* in three tiers, look decidedly 17th-century.

The walls of the first-floor **Gallery** are lined with a collection of 325 portraits of famous men and women grouped by date in panels and running from Philippe VI de Valois (1328–50) and Edward III of England to Louis XIII (1610–43) and Charles I. The latest information suggests these were commissioned in 1676 from one of the sons of the painter Jean Mosnier. The panelling below is inset with allegorical paintings inspired by contemporary emblematic books. These portrait galleries were very much a 17th-century phenomenon—among the best known examples is that created by Bussy Rabutin during his exile to his château in Burgundy in the 1660s.

The château was acquired in 1617 by Paul Ardier, Contrôleur des Guerres, who ten years later received from the Netherlands, presumably from Delft, a large quantity of blue and white tiles depicting a detailed

Bird's-eye view of Beauregard from the north by du Cerceau.

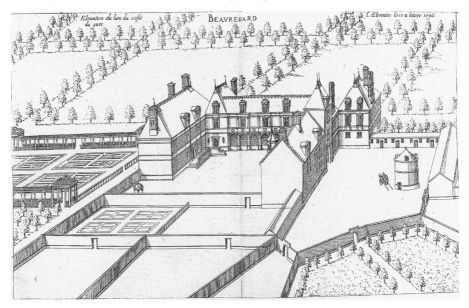

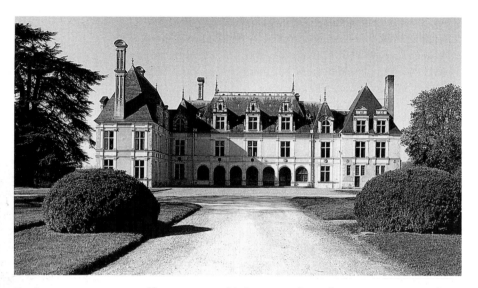

The Renaissance entrance courtyard at Beauregard.

military scene of infantry and cavalry—*toute une armée en marche*. These were finally in place on the gallery floor in 1646; the present owners have recently found a cache of unused tiles—this explains why some are virtually unworn.

BLOIS

Arriving at Blois by car, you might conclude that the roads around it were designed for a new version of the Monte Carlo Rally. While circling precipitously you will see the great loggias of the François I wing and to the right the massive white stone palace begun by Gaston d'Orléans. If you make your way to the *place* to the east of the château, you will find a less portentous entrance range in red brick—the Louis XII wing built in 1498–1501.

To the right of this wing is a large plain hall with a gabled roof, known as the **Salle des États Généraux** (the States-General met here twice, in 1576 and 1588). This is the main survival of the medieval château of the Counts of Blois and was certainly the work of Thibaud VI who died in 1218. The enceinte of the château must have reached its present proportions in the 13th or 14th century. Froissart, the great chronicler of the Hundred Years War, called it one of the finest châteaux in the kingdom.

In 1498 the Count of Blois, Louis d'Orléans, suddenly became King of France on the death of his cousin Charles VIII at Amboise. The new King Louis XII had been brought up at Blois and so installed his court here. The brick buildings he constructed on three sides of the courtyard are recorded in another of du Cerceau's bird's-eye views.

Much of the diapered brickwork on the entrance front has the hard look of 19th-century restoration, and the stonework alas is distinctly dirty. Look more closely and the detail is ravishing and will gradually be revealed in the vast programme of repairs now underway.

The arcade in the courtyard heralds the arrival of the Renaissance: classical details are now mingled with Gothic. Here are the first, rather stout, classical columns—alternately circular and square, or rather diamond-shaped, their shafts richly carved with lattice patterns. To the left is part of **Louis XII's South Wing** and behind it the choir of his chapel consecrated in 1508 (the nave was demolished in the 17th century by Gaston d'Orléans). The crucial innovation of Louis XII's work is that it is without towers or battlements or drawbridges and has large windows looking outwards. He was constructing a palace not a fortress.

François I, on becoming King in 1515, immediately

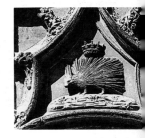

(Above) Blois: Louis XII's symbol of the porcupine.

(Below) View of Blois in the 16th century by du Cerceau.

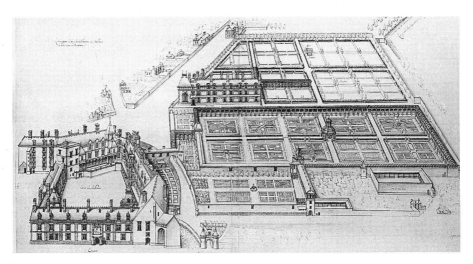

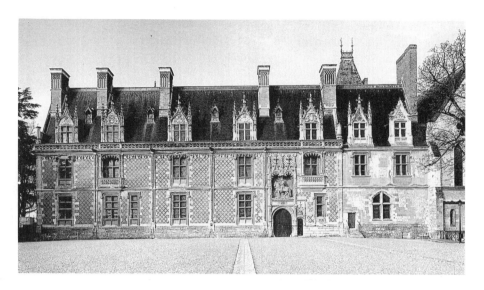

The entrance range at Blois built for Louis XII.

embarked on building at Blois and the difference in style between this work and that of Louis XII, although only separated by 15 years, could not be more marked. The shape and design of François' buildings were nonetheless substantially determined by his decision to use the foundations—and incorporate the walls—of the medieval north range. Even the great Renaissance staircase in the courtyard replaced a tower of roughly the same shape.

Overlooking the town, the new loggias, and the rooms behind, probably built after 1520, are built out in front of three medieval towers. The outline of one of these is clearly visible on the right. As a result the **François I façades** are not regular: some arches are divided by single pilasters, others by double, or by two pilasters framing a niche. Perhaps the most remarkable aspect of the outer front is the way the King built out in front of the rock face necessitating, to the left, a vast substructure to support his new loggias. Arcaded loggias had already been used—in Gothic form—at Amboise and Gaillon, but at Blois there are two levels of arcades, with a third consisting of short paired columns carrying a straight lintel—exactly what is found in Florentine Renaissance palaces. The source here appears to be the famous Raphael loggias in the Vatican, only finished in 1519. However at Blois the loggias are not true arcades, but just deep window recesses suggesting the designers were working from rather sketchy drawings or descriptions.

François I's architect is unknown; it could have been Domenico da Cortona, who had been brought back by Charles VIII from Italy and who lived at Blois from 1512 to 1530. More probably it was the mason Jacques Sourdeau whose name is recorded here in 1516 and 1518, and who became master of works for the *comté* of Blois in 1519, and was in charge of the masonry at Chambord between 1519–21.

The *tour de force* of François' work is unquestionably the great octagonal **Stair** in the courtyard which brings a new monumentality to French architecture. Open stairs like this were not new in France—there is one in the famous mid-15th-century house of Jacques Coeur at Bourges. Here the stonework has an altogether greater sense of mass and depth. An extraordinary dynamism and tension develops as the balconies, arches and cornices (and handrail inside) all rise at different angles—shallow outside, steep within. And as you ascend, the serpentine shape of the steps heightens the feeling that everything is on the move. The new monumentality is also evident in

Blois: the arcaded galleries overlooking the town added by François I.

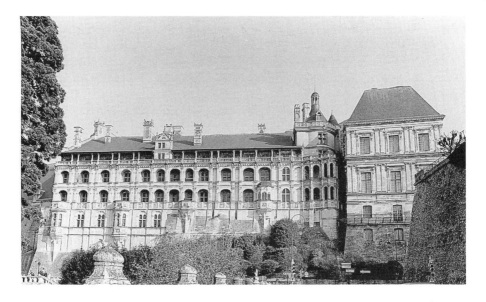

45

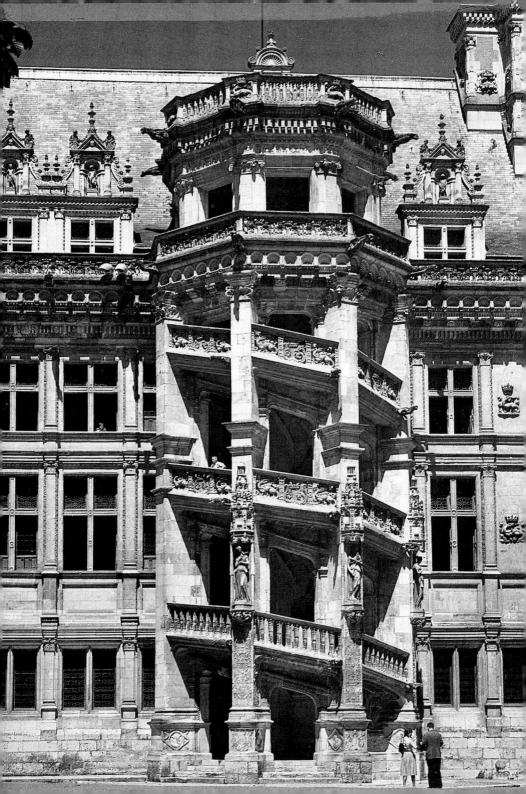

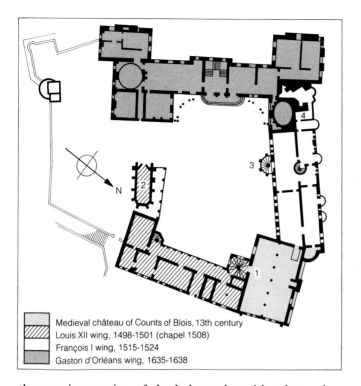

Blois: plan of the first storey
1. Salle des Etats
   Généraux
2. Chapel
3. Stair
4. Cabinet

N

Medieval château of Counts of Blois, 13th century
Louis XII wing, 1498-1501 (chapel 1508)
François I wing, 1515-1524
Gaston d'Orléans wing, 1635-1638

the massive carving of the balustrades with salamanders and scrolls entirely filling the panels.

The interiors of the **François I Wing** are not what you would expect. Be prepared to enter a 19th-century world of make-believe as rich and opulent, and almost as imaginative, as the famous contemporary interiors by William Burges at Cardiff Castle in Wales. The highly colourful decoration is almost entirely the result of restoration undertaken by Felix Duban in 1845–8 and deserves to be more highly regarded (and fully acknowledged) than it is at present. His polychrome decorations consist of richly painted and gilt wall hangings, murals and stencils—a complete showcase of 19th-century decorative techniques, most of spirited quality, and still strong in colour.

The first room has a sumptuous François I chimneypiece, richly polychromed and gilded by Duban, and a wonderfully idiosyncratic Renaissance doorway which

(Opposite) Blois: the monumental octagonal staircase in the courtyard added by François I.

expresses inexhaustible delight in the new decorative vocabulary. The other principal 16th-century survival is the panelled **Cabinet** with 237 panels (try finding a repeat). Secret doors are opened by levers concealed in the skirting. Now that the tour is without a guide, you are no longer subject to a prolonged re-enactment of the murder of the Duc de Guise by Henry III, but, if you can, make a point of reading the gripping description in Ian Dunlop's book *Châteaux of the Loire*.

The decoration of the 13th-century **Salle des États Généraux** is again wholly the work of Duban, dating from 1861–6. The scale of this room for its date is awe-inspiring. The roofs stencilled with gold fleurs-de-lis on a blue ground are like the upturned hulls of two wooden ships, supported down the middle of the room by columns carrying pointed arches. The walls are painted to suggest stonework with imitation hangings below looking rather like gilt-embossed leather.

The next treat is the **Gaston d'Orléans Wing** at the end of the courtyard. Though Duc d'Orléans, Gaston preferred Blois, and in 1634 he was effectively exiled here on account of his constant intrigues at Court. His architect was the young François Mansart, today the most highly regarded of all French classical architects, who produced designs for a vast new palace around a courtyard, larger and more monumental than the Palais de Luxembourg. This would have required the demolition of all the other buildings on the site, as well as massive substructures to support symmetrical wings which would have projected well beyond the existing rock. By 1638 work had come to a complete halt, whether because Gaston could no longer pay the bills, or because the birth of Louis XIV (in September 1638) spelt the end of his hopes of the throne, is not clear. For this one can only breathe a sigh of relief.

Mansart's work is nonetheless of surpassing quality, and in the courtyard at Blois one can learn as much about classical architecture as anywhere in France. And the contrast of styles between the ornate Renaissance work of François I and the more restrained 17th-century classicism does not jar: rather the juxtaposition of two such masterpieces heightens the experience. Mansart eschews a

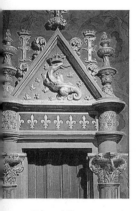

(Above) Renaissance doorway in the François I wing.

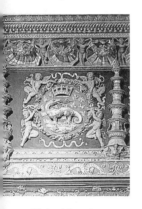

(Below) Renaissance overmantel in the François I wing, painted and gilded in the mid-19th century.

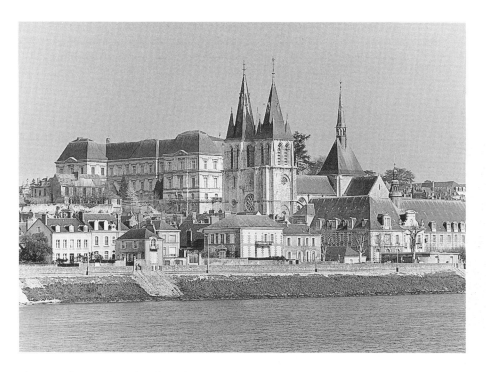

giant order and maintains the Renaissance formula of
Doric, Ionic and Corinthian applied in sequence to each
floor. His genius lies in avoiding monotony and building
up rhythms and climaxes toward the centre and sides of
the building. By this date the riot of carved ornament
prevalent a century before had been eliminated and the
emphasis was instead on chasteness and correctness.

On the ground floor he uses full columns, in pairs, to
frame the entrance and to create quadrant colonnades,
softening the corners. On the first floor the pairs of Ionic
columns are restricted to the central windows, forming
with those below, a centrepiece within a centrepiece. On
the upper floor the central bay is emphasized by the
shallowest of forward breaks in the cornice, which makes
an explosive upward surge to contain a shield with the
fleurs-de-lis of France, flanked by trophies of armour and
flags.

The final vertical thrust comes with the extra height of
the whole centrepiece—the full entablature oversails that

Blois: view across the
Loire to the château
showing the Gaston
d'Orléans wing
added by François
Mansart (1635–38).

of the bays to the sides. Mansart creates this difference of levels in the top storey by using shorter pilasters at the sides, without full Corinthian capitals and without a full entablature.

When work came to a halt in 1638 Mansart's wing had neither floors nor a staircase—Gaston passed the rest of his life (he died in 1660), admiring his work from the François I wing.

The actual staircase was only inserted in 1932 on the model of that in Mansart's château at Maisons-Lafitte near Paris. Notwithstanding this, Mansart's staircase hall is one of the great architectual spaces of western secular architecture providing a view upwards akin to the crossing of a great cathedral. Here you view a dome, entirely constructed of stone, floating ethereally, for the means of support—the arches and the pendentives—are concealed from view by a gallery in the shape of a shallow cross. The gallery is of even more massive monumentality with profuse, deeply undercut enrichments. The carving is attributed to Simon Guillain, assisted by the young sculptor Michel Anguier. Look at the walls however and you will see the programme is incomplete: large rectangular blocks await the sculptor's chisel.

If, on leaving, you walk out to the right and admire the view from the terrace over the Loire you can also see how Mansart used a full Corinthian order and entablature on the upper storey all round the outer face of the Orléans wing. Here he had to tackle the greatest tease facing a classical architect—how to adapt the Ionic captial, which is essentially like a scroll of parchment, to inside and outside corners. Mansart juxtaposes the front and side views of the capitals on the outside corners, while on the inside ones, two capitals simply melt together.

A model on display in the chapel also shows how the centres of the two fronts of Mansart's wing are not aligned—a point concealed within by the staircase.

BONHÔTEL   This château is Loire Revival *par excellence*. One can imagine it standing at Newport, Rhode Island, or even on Fifth Avenue in New York. Here are all the fairy-tale elements that appealed to 19th-century magnates: turrets, belvederes, gables and soaring chimneys, all intended to proclaim power and pedigree (see photograph on p.28).

The give-away as to its date is the *porte-cochère*, clearly integral to the design, and an essential component of a grand 19th-century house built for entertainment, and of course, the built-in folding metal shutters.

Bonhôtel was built between 1875–82 for M. du Pré de Saint-Maur, by the architects Louis and Clement Parent, best known for their Parisian hôtels. For all the fantasy of its silhouette, it is strictly symmetrical in plan. The bartisans (projecting turrets) at the corners have blind battlements as well as turrets; over the porch there is a squared ogee roof and to the side a tapering one. Inside there is a two-storey, arcaded stone hall.

The château is private, but a fair view of it can be obtained from the gate. The house looks down to a lake, while across the road is another large lake with a boat house.

Bonhôtel is marked on the Michelin map by a white rectangle just west of Ligny-le-Ribault, which is some 25 km (16 miles) SSW of Orléans along the D 15.

Brissac towers above low-lying fields and vineyards, its massive height accentuated by steep roofs and a forest of slender chimneys held precariously in position by iron rods.

BRISSAC

Some find Brissac's extraordinary entrance front clumsy or even disconcerting; but to me the restless classical façade cramped between two massive medieval towers, speaks more strongly and splendidly of a great and continuing ancestral domain than any other château on the Loire.

The towers were built by Pierre de Brézé, minister of Charles VII and Louis XI, who was killed in 1465 during the insurrection against Louis XI known as the Ligue du Bien Public. They have the massive two-stage tops of the towers at Langeais, but the wall-walks are faced with rich Gothic panelling.

In 1502 Pierre's nephew sold the estate to René de

Brissac: the ambitious early 17th-century château, begun in 1606, remains framed by the mid-15th-century towers.

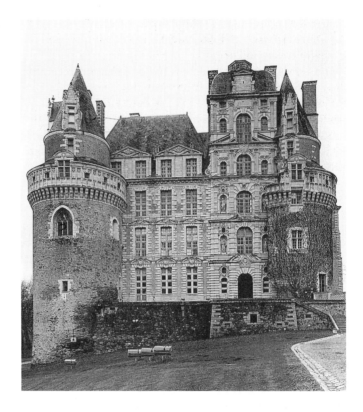

Cossé, Chamberlain of Charles VIII. Among his descendants were four marshals of France. The first was his son Charles for whom Brissac was raised to the title of Count, the second, Charles II de Cossé, was the Governor of Paris who opened the gates of the capital to Henri IV, in 1594. Twelve years later Brissac was raised to a Duchy.

In 1606 Charles II de Cossé embarked on the construction of a vast new château on a quadrilateral plan, corresponding to his rank as one of the great men of France. In the event only part of the entrance range was built with the staircase tower, crowned by an imperial dome, crushed uncomfortably against a 14th-century tower. His master mason Jacques Corbineau evidently had a horror of empty walls: the front, in Ian Dunlop's felicitous phrase, has 'the scintillating, many-faceted appearance of a cut-glass decanter'.

The five storeys of the **Staircase Tower** represent the five orders of architecture. At the lowest level the Tuscan pilasters are totally imprisoned in banded stonework so that only the capitals and bases are visible; above, the pilasters (Doric, Ionic, Corinthian, composite) are progressively liberated. Charles II de Cossé's high office is trumpeted by treating each level as a triumphal arch, with a central arch flanked by small round-headed windows or niches; unity is achieved by the use of broken pediments that fly open like a series of double doors.

To the left of the staircase tower, the windows are all linked vertically in the manner characteristic of Henri IV and Louis XIII with pronounced alternating quoins, but each level is treated differently. The first level has segmental pediments, the second triangular ones, the third banded arches, whereas at the top, in another curious and original piece of Mannerist eccentricity, the pedimented dormers are paired beneath a single larger pediment. Everywhere the carving is astonishly rich: shell-headed niches, cartouches, garlands, swags, coats of arms and military trophies abound. Beside the front door note the original octagonal and square leaded glazing in the small arched windows.

Be sure to walk round to view the château from the park. Here you will see the massive artificial platform on which it is constructed as well as more of Corbineau's restless masonry overlooking the garden terrace—a triple arcade, triple as well as double dormers and a crowd of *oeil-de-bœuf* windows.

The death of the first Duc de Brissac in 1621 brought the project to a halt. His son Louis chose to extend the house with a new wing, even taller (measured from the ground) to the right of the entrance front.

Inside, Brissac is full of atmosphere, as evocative and complete an early 17th-century ensemble as Ham House on the outskirts of London, or Skokloster outside Stockholm. As in a great Venetian *palazzo*, the stone hall is very much a continuation of the outside architecture, with magnificent stone doorcases carrying resplendent coats of arms, the carving of which (protected as it is from the elements) is still in pristine condition.

The **Grand Salon** to the left has a sumptuous, richly sculpted and gilded open-beam ceiling with a vast stone chimneypiece containing a bust of the first Duke. Note the way the windows are divided into eight squares, each with its own shutter painted front and back. The 18th-century Gobelin tapestries portray framed oil paintings surrounded by garlands of flowers.

Opposite, the **Dining-Room** has a musicians' gallery approached by twin curving stairs, all cleverly painted in imitation of marble. On the adjoining wall is what must be one of the largest country-house views ever painted, portraying the arrival of the Duc and Duchesse de Maine at the Château de Bercy in the Val-de-Marne. Alas this magnificent house was entirely demolished in 1861 and its *boiseries* dispersed to Paris and even England, though some of the contents including portraits came to Brissac.

Ancient, well-worn floors give a wonderful feel of authenticity to any building and Brissac has an abundance—the stone floors on the landings as well as in the main rooms like the 30–metre (32–yd) long **Salle des Gardes** (here in the form of a long gallery) are of many different patterns; elsewhere there are brick-tiled and herringbone wooden floors. The bedrooms with their huge tapestries, *armoires* and richly painted 17th-century ceilings are full of atmosphere, though seeing how tapestries were cut to fit invariably causes surprise and even pain. In the **Chambre de Louis XIII** the window reveals have recently been repainted following the original scheme. Note in particular the numerous painted panels on the ceiling beams in the main rooms.

The tour of Brissac has an unexpected climax, a magnificent **Theatre** on the second floor. This was built in 1890 specially for the Marquise de Brissac, a friend of Gounod, Saint-Saëns and Debussy, who regularly sang in operas herself. The theatre has recently been handsomely restored by the friends of the château.

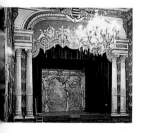

Brissac: the 1890 theatre.

BURY

The remains of Bury are very fragmentary but nonetheless highly evocative. Its importance as one of the very first examples of the Loire Renaissance style was recognized and recorded by du Cerceau in two superbly detailed bird's-eye views showing the château from both east and west.

Bury was built for a rich courtier, Florimond Robertet, who was one of the principal counsellors and financial secretaries of three kings—Charles VIII, Louis XII and François I. In Blois he built the magnificent Hôtel d'Alluye, which the Florentine ambassador described in 1508 as newly constructed. This has a glorious arcaded courtyard with classical detail, but arches bearing a trace of Gothic. Deeds show that Robertet bought the land at Bury from Germanin de Bonneval for 4,000 gold crowns on 2 January 1511, and states that the old *château fort* was *'en ruyne'*. The initial L on the façade suggests that the new château was well advanced by January 1515.

Bury, with Azay-le-Rideau and Chenonceau, anticipates stylistically the great building work that François I began on his accession in 1515 when classical detail was introduced on a large scale. Bury was important for the new regularity of its plan—the layout being divided into

View of Bury by du Cerceau, recording the early 16th-century house and formal garden.

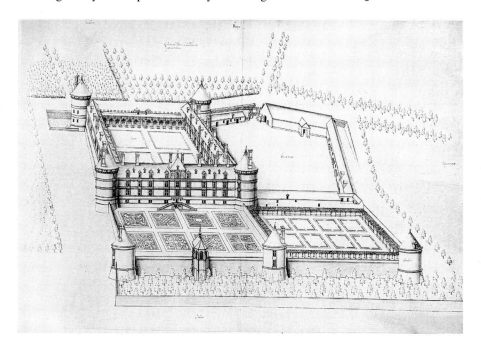

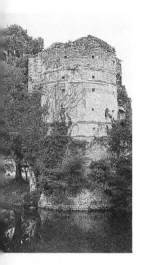

Bury: only fragments remain including this tower.

four roughly even rectangles. The main axis was continued across the *cour d'honneur* in the garden and terminated by a chapel. The entrance range on the inside had a full classical arcade with 'correct' semi-circular arches (as opposed to the flattened arches often used in the late Gothic period), and the *corps-de-logis* had the arrangement of windows framed by pilasters, strong horizontal courses and elaborate dormers that were the hallmarks of the Loire style. Traces of this detail can be seen on the surviving towers, still bathed by the moats shown by du Cerceau. The use of towers in one sense makes Bury more medieval (Azay and Chenonceau only have turrets at the corners), but large round *poivrières* continued to be a signature of château architecture all over France well into the 18th century—witness in particular Montgeoffroy near Angers.

The designer of Bury remains unknown though it has been attributed to Fra Giocondo, while others have suggested a resemblance to the work of Giuliano da Sangallo. It seems more likely that it is the work of a French master mason strongly influenced by Italian ideas.

The château passed in 1604 to the Villeroys, then to the Rostaings, and fell into ruin between 1666 and 1734.

CHAMBORD

To call Chambord 'a hunting lodge' is like describing St Peter's as an oratory. Here is an expression of the French concept of monarchy as remarkable and fascinating as Versailles. And while Versailles speaks of absolutism and was intended to reduce the entire French artistocracy to the level of court functionaries whose humiliation extended to the point that there was nowhere except the corridors to relieve themselves, Chambord is a nobler embodiment of the ideals of kingship.

The latest research and analysis by the French scholars Jean Guillaume and J. Martin-Demezil convincingly attribute the concept and design to Leonardo, who François I had brought to France and installed at the Manoir du Clos-Lucé, near Amboise, from 1516 until his death in 1519.

Chambord brings an altogether new monumentality to

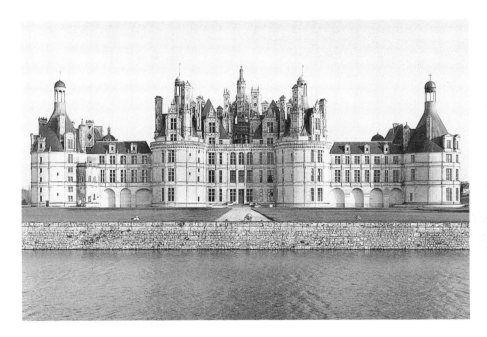

French architecture: here is a building which in the formality and extent of its layout, the symmetry of its parts, its strongly architectural character inside as well as out, is a secular cathedral, proclaiming the ascent of temporal power over that of the church.

Kings, of course, have always sought to establish their lineage, as part of their right to power, and for this reason Chambord architecturally looks back as well as forward. The astonishing silhouette is as rich, indeed richer than all the chivalrous show of the late medieval castles in *Les Très Riches Heures du Duc de Berry*. The central *donjon*—with its four circular towers—looks back to the soaring *donjon* of another great royal castle, the 14th-century Château de Vincennes. The huge round corner towers have the dimensions of those of *châteaux forts*— not the tourelles of Azay-le-Rideau and Chenonceau, which are Chambord's immediate precursors. Yet despite the archaic style, the architectural vocabulary is classical, the detail not only Italian, but of purer Italian design than had so far been seen in France. François I's sister wrote to him apropos of Chambord:

Chambord: the north front begun in 1519.

57

To see your building without you, is to see a corpse. To look at it without hearing your intentions is like reading in Hebrew.

François I's initial idea had been to rebuild the Château of Romorantin to the south-east, which belonged to Louise of Savoy but the project was abandoned due to the plague, and Chambord, the medieval château of the Counts of Blois, in the midst of a vast forest, was chosen instead.

François I ascended the throne in 1515, and plans were evidently advanced when, on 6 September 1519, he appointed a *surintendant* of building works, François de Pontbrient. The master masons were Jacques Sourdeau of Loches (from 1519 until his death in 1522); then Pierre Nepveu dit Trinqueau of Amboise (from 1522 until his death in 1538); and Jacques Coqueau of Blois (from 1537 until his death in 1569). No mention of an architect is made in the documents. Domenico da Cortona, who had been brought back from Italy by Charles VIII, acted as both model-maker and, on occasion, architect for François I. He made several models of châteaux, bridges and mills for the King from 1517 onwards. Cortona's wooden

Chambord: plan of the ground floor

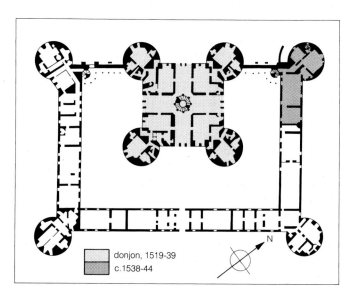

donjon, 1519-39
c.1538-44

model of Chambord was drawn by the architect André Félibien about 1680 when it was evidently in a very poor state, being shown without its roofs or wings.

The model shows a much more Italianate design than that of the completed building with 'pure' round-headed arcades on three floors. Internally, the design prefigures Chambord's highly unusual Greek cross plan (with equal arms), though the staircase, unlike the one actually built, is of the straight enclosed type, doubling back on itself.

Chambord's unusual plan is however that proposed (but not executed) by Leonardo da Vinci for the Milanese villa of Charles d'Amboise. Leonardo also made numerous drawings experimenting with double stairs (some of them reputedly for bordellos, to ensure that the customers coming in did not meet those going out). Leonardo was also constantly experimenting with drawings of centrally planned churches, with richly modelled silhouettes, which are not very far removed from Chambord's lantern tower. These circular spiral stairs can equally be said to be of French origin, and there was a medieval precedent for the double ramp in the Bernadine College in Paris.

The building of Chambord spanned a very long period and a detailed chronology would be tedious here, but there was a complete break in work from June 1524 to October 1526, during François I's captivity in Italy. A capital of the lantern tower is dated 1533, and in 1541 there are payments for gilding the leadwork of the roof. The east wing was under construction in 1539 and the west in 1550. After François I's death in 1547 work continued at a reduced level, but later capitals still carry his salamander.

Unlike Henry VIII's contemporary palace at Nonsuch in Surrey, which was so ignominiously destroyed during the Commonwealth, Chambord retained its importance and prestige in succeeding centuries. Gaston d'Orléans, who lived at Blois from 1626 until his death in 1660, was fond of Chambord, and restored the lantern towers. Louis XIV came regularly to hunt; he relinquished the François I wing to reside in the first floor of the north-east tower. In 1687–85 J.H. Mansart, architect of Versailles, was commissioned to carry out extensive repairs and a plan

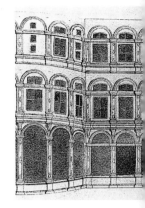

Detail of sketch made by Félibien about 1680 of the model of Chambord executed about 1519 by Domenico da Cortona. The model had apparently lost its roof.

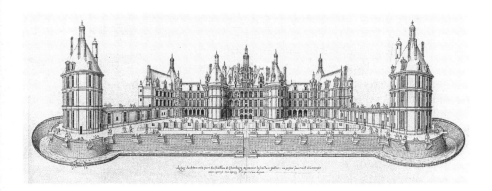

Chambord: view by du Cerceau of the proposed arrangement of the entrance courtyard.

attributed to him, proposes moats all around the château as well as extensive *parterres*.

Between 1725 and 1733 Stanislas Leszczynski, the exiled King of Poland, resided at Chambord, and later Marshal Saxe. The furniture was dispersed—or pillaged during the Revolution—but in 1806 Napoleon granted the château to Marshal Berthier.

Chambord and its park were classified as Monuments Historiques in 1840 and extensive repairs were carried out by the architects Desbois, father and son, for the Comte de Chambord and his Bourbon-Parme nephews. After neglect during the First World War, Chambord was acquired by the state in 1930, and major works of repair, decoration and furnishing are currently in progress.

The layout of Chambord consists of a square *donjon* with circular corner towers, enclosed in a larger rectangular courtyard with matching towers at the corners. Those on the entrance rise to first floor level. The three low wings of offices were added under J.H. Mansart in the 1680s. Two engravings by du Cerceau record the project as conceived about 1526 and show the entire castle surrounded by a continuous terrace and moat. At that time it was intended the courtyard should be open on the approach.

Though the château appears symmetrical, closer inspection reveals considerable variations in the windows and the roofscape. One unexpected solecism in the long regular garden front is the way in which the second tower from the left is turned 45° out of alignment with the

others. François I perhaps liked to test his guests' powers
of observation.

Chambord, like Chenonceau, is overwhelmed with
visitors, so it is worth arriving early and making the ascent
of the glorious stair so you have the roof to yourself. The
roof terraces at Chambord rank among the most magical
creations of western architecture. It is like a town in
miniature complete with streets and houses. The fantasy is
pure Flamboyant Gothic, transformed into a Renaissance
vision of the ideal city, in which chimneys become towers,
and cupolas belfries. Here is the perfect place to absorb
the vocabulary of the early French Renaissance: panelled
pilasters, tapering pediments, shell-headed arches and
niches, candelabra, stone-roofed cupolas, gabled chim-
ney-tops like miniature sarcophagi. Here almost for the
first time extensive use is made of full columns rather than
flat pilasters. Most fantastic of all is the central lantern
with tier upon tier as in a wedding cake. In all there are
five stages, sharply diminishing in scale towards the top.

Internally, Chambord is like no other royal palace: you
have the feeling of walking around the triforium (upper
arcade) of a cathedral looking down at the crossing. The

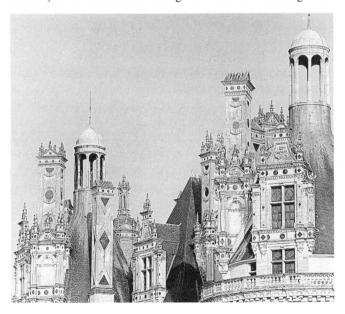

Chambord: close-up
view of the dormers,
chimneys and
cupolas.

matching arms of the Greek cross with their deeply coffered elliptical vaults are as bare and empty as the refectories of some long abandoned abbey, but they have huge fireplaces and it is evident that the building was conceived, like the Paris Opera, to be constantly thronged with people in gorgeous finery, continuously moving up and down to different levels. In the vaults, alas, you can see all too well the damage done to the superb carving by leaking roofs. Nonetheless, what remains has a plasticity and high relief that speaks of a new monumentality arrived from Italy.

The corners of the Greek cross are arranged into apartments (with a second apartment in the towers beyond) and in recent years there has been a sustained programme to recreate the formality and splendour of the state bedrooms and give the smaller rooms a more intimate feel with pretty chintzes.

The **King's Apartment** shows the characteristic theatrical arrangement for the *levée*, with the bed set in a recess and framed by what is, in effect, a proscenium arch with a balustrade almost like an altar rail, as if to emphasize the divinity of kings and keep all but a favoured few away from the Royal Person.

To my mind the most evocative of these rooms is the **Chambre de Monseigneur le Dauphin** on the first floor. This is a 19th-century room with rich heavy hangings, dedicated to the Comte de Chambord, with a massive state bed (never used) signed Emile Poinçon, Nantes, 1873.

Chambord is often photographed reflected in the water, but you must walk quite a distance behind the château to obtain this view. At the beginning of this century the landscape architect Achille Duchêne made designs for surrounding the château with a moat, as originally intended, with formal gardens set on a large island platform. In the event only the further arm was constructed by canalizing the Cosson.

CHAMEROLLES

Chamerolles represents a phenomenon unthinkable in many countries: a major rescue and restoration of a château in a desperate state, accompanied by a pioneering

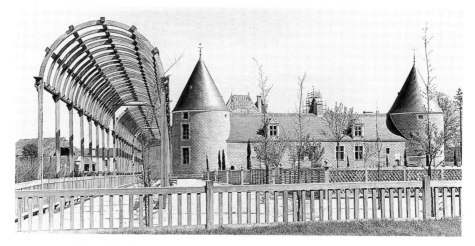

reconstruction of its Renaissance gardens, all initiated and funded by local government.

The château stands at the north of the forest of Orléans very close to the road. It was built for Lancelot du Lac, Chamberlain of Louis XII and Governor of Orléans, who died here in 1522. His grandson, also Lancelot, was a Protestant and Chamerolles became a part of the Protestant defences of Orléans. In the chapel the altar was suppressed and the retable replaced by a painted decalogue. This has recently been re-exposed.

Chamerolles changed hands several times in succeeding centuries. From 1900 the château was by degrees abandoned and its interior systematically pillaged until 1987 when it was acquired by the Département of Loiret. Restoration of both house and gardens has been entrusted to Jacques Moulin, architecte en chef des Monuments Historiques, assisted by Brigitte Barbier and de Thierry Gilson, landscape architects. It is planned that the château will be completed and opened to the public in the summer of 1991.

The château is laid out on a characteristic square plan with circular corner towers and a central square entrance tower flanked by turrets. Though the departmental archives were burnt in June 1940, documents have been found in the Archives Nationales showing that the garden was divided into six squares, two planted with vegetables.

Chamerolles: photograph taken during reconstruction of the gardens of the early 16th-century château.

The planting of the *parterres* has been modelled on views of contemporary gardens by du Cerceau and on gardens shown in tapestries, and each square is laid out on a different plan. Particularly impressive are the long wooden pergolas on either side. M. Moulin has also designed the **Kiosk au Miroir** at the top of the lake to the south. For anyone interested in the restoration of formal gardens Chamerolles is a must.

CHAMPIGNY-SUR-VEUDE

The Château de Champigny is no more; it was demolished by Cardinal Richelieu after he acquired the property in 1635 because, it is said, Champigny vied with the château Richelieu was himself constructing nearby (poetic justice, of a rather unfortunate kind, came with the destruction of the Château de Richelieu in the Revolution).

Louis I de Bourbon inherited a château dating from the 13th century in the 1470s. The new château was probably more the work of his son, Louis II, who inherited in 1520, and even more of his wife, Jacqueline de Longwy, who he married in 1538. She was one of the great ladies of Renaissance letters, and niece of the Cardinal de Givry, a humanist and amateur architect.

A view of 1699 by Gaignières shows the position of the demolished château beyond the *avant-cour*, surrounded on three sides by the *communs*. These were remodelled as a residence by La Grande Demoiselle, daughter of Gaston d'Orléans, after she gained possession of the property in 1656.

The corner towers of the surviving *communs*, with their bulbous domes, recall Valençay and suggest a date in the 1540s. The **Pavillon de Jupiter**, an entrance pavilion in the form of a triumphal arch, dates from the second half of the century. Inside there are still ribbed vaults (late for this date), as well as a Renaissance chimneypiece and one added by La Grande Demoiselle.

Champigny-sur-Veude: view by Gaignières (1699) showing the site of the demolished château in the trees behind the *avant-cour*.

The spectacular collegiate chapel, which is open to the public, is a parallel to that at Ussé. The style is still Gothic; work apparently began in 1508 and the chapel was dedicated in 1545. The chapel was dedicated to the memory of Saint Louis, ancestor of Louis I de Bourbon.

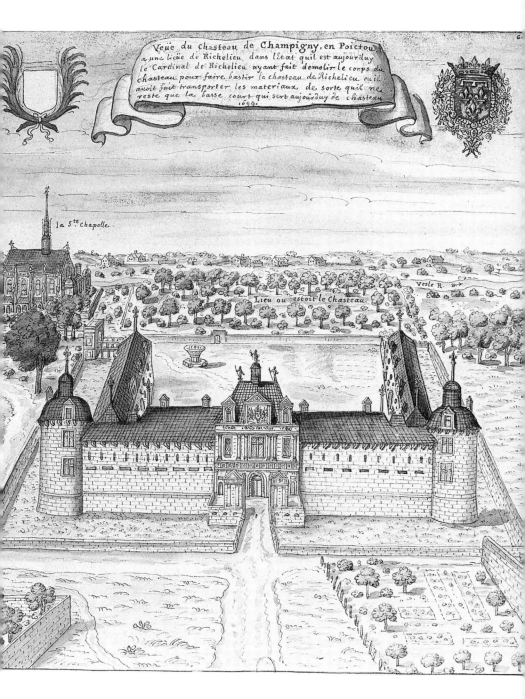

Veüe du chasteau de Champigny, en Poictou à une Lieüe de Richelieu, dans l'Etat qu'il est aujourduy le Cardinal de Richelieu ayant fait demolir le corps du chasteau pour faire bastir le chasteau de Richelieu ou il auoit fait transporter les materiaux, de sorte qu'il ne reste que la basse court qui sert aujourduy de chasteau 1699.

la S.te Chapelle.

Vesle R.

Lieu ou estoit le Chasteau

Champigny-sur-
Veude: the entrance.

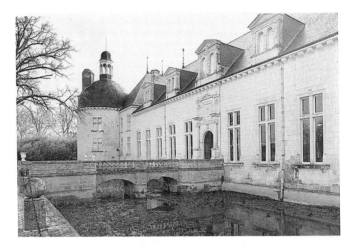

The most remarkable element is the chapel's Renaissance vestibule added about 1550 or soon after, the work of the mason Toussaint Chesneau. With an open arched front it has overtones of the Pazzi chapel in Florence, but the most outstanding part is the internal hall, all in masonry, with two orders of columns, very rich entablatures and niches. The treatment is that of an immensely rich architectural casket, with a barrel-vaulted roof that might unhinge. The architect of this work is unknown, but it is of the quality of the architect Philibert de L'Orme (the first French architect to compare with the great Italians), or could indeed be by an Italian.

CHANTELOUP

The great château of the Duc de Choiseul was demolished in the 1820s and the elaborate gardens have long since vanished, but his remarkable pagoda survives and is well worth a visit by anyone who delights in follies.

Choiseul had bought the estate in 1761. A protegé of Madame de Pompadour, he was between 1758 and 1770 successively Minister of Foreign Affairs, of War and of the Navy. In 1768 he negotiated the acquisition of Corsica.

Not surprisingly, he sought to make a princely residence of Chanteloup, and commissioned the architect Le Camus de Mezières to extend the château with colonnades, pavilions and vast *communs*, enriching the interior with magnificent collections and furnishings. Madame du Barry, however, turned against him and obtained his dismissal in 1770, and he retired to Chanteloup to hold court—providing the model, it is said, for Beaumarchais' *Marriage of Figaro*. Disgrace came with the death of Louis XV in 1774.

Chanteloup's pagoda was begun on 3 September 1773 and completed five years later on 28 April 1778. The comparison is often made with the pagoda built by Sir William Chambers at Kew Gardens beside the river Thames, but there are important distinctions between the two in both landscape setting and design.

Firstly, Choiseul did not abandon French formality for the *sharawadgi* or wiggly lines seen in the English version of a Chinese garden. His pagoda stood on the axis of the château at a point where seven avenues through the forest of Amboise converged. It also looked down on a semi-circular mirror of water continued from the centre as a grand canal. The Chinese element of the garden was tucked away to one side where it would not disturb the symmetry; its winding paths, bulbous rocks and sinuous brooks were contained within rectangular boundaries.

Secondly, whereas Chambers' pagoda at Kew is Chinese in detail as well as design, Le Camus' pagoda transpires, at close quarters, to be entirely classical, without oriental trim of any kind. It consists of seven stages, set back one above another. The lowest are circular, those above, octagonal. The ground floor colonnade is in the form of a *tholos* with the baseless Greek Doric columns which are a hallmark of full neo-classicism. The pagoda element comes from the concave sweep of the shallow roofs and the geometric patterns of the iron-work—akin to the fretwork patterns of Chinese Chippendale. Part of the delight of the pagoda is to experience the ingenious way the staircase is contrived in ever more constricted spaces. Choiseul conceived his pagoda as a Temple of Friendship: on the base are inscribed *Reconnaissance* and *Amitié*.

An excellent exhibition on Chanteloup and 18th-century gardening has been installed in a pavilion at the entrance.

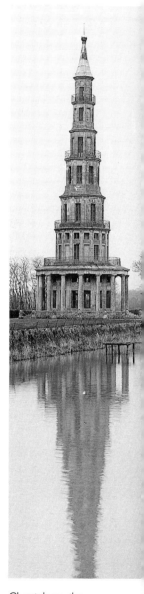

Chanteloup: the pagoda.

CHAUMONT   Seen from across the Loire, Chaumont makes a perfect picture. The château stands at the top of a green escarpment, embowered by trees; below, village houses form a picturesque line along the river looking down to the water over a continuous smooth green verge. You can either walk up from the village, or drive round to the entrance on the south. As you come closer to the château the grass and trees so soften the mighty towers that it seems almost like a park ornament. This is partly because the landscape conceals the height of the castle walls; you approach at the level of the drawbridge which is set well above the foot of the flanking towers.

A look-out post had been established here at the end of the tenth century, by the Counts of Blois, to guard against Angevin raiding parties. A century later Chaumont passed to the Amboise family, and in 1465 Louis XI ordered the demolition of the château to punish Pierre d'Amboise for taking part in the rebellion known as the Ligue du Bien Public. Soon after, however, he returned to favour and was able to begin the reconstruction of the château on the present quadrilateral plan.

By his death in 1473 he had completed the now vanished north range and the existing west wing and large Tour d'Amboise at the south-west corner. The task of completion fell, however, to his grandson Charles II d'Amboise, who inherited in 1481, and also carried out a major remodelling of the Château de Meillant in Berry between 1500–10.

Charles II was Grand Maître de la Maison du Roi, Marshal and Admiral of France, and was made Governor of Milan by Louis XII. As he was so much in Italy it is thought the building works at Chaumont were entrusted to his uncle, the celebrated Cardinal d'Amboise, first Minister to Louis XII, who was at this time transforming the Château de Gaillon in Normandy into the masterpiece of the early French Renaissance.

Between 1498 and 1510 the south and east ranges were added, with windows that are still Gothic in detail, completing the quadrangle—a building join can clearly be seen on the south front. The entrance towers are adorned

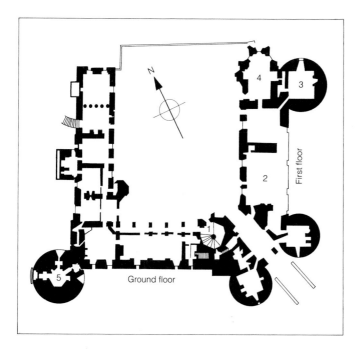

Chaumont
1. Staircase
2. Council chamber
3. Astrologer's room
4. Chapel
5. Tour d'Amboise

with a frieze of interlaced C's for Charles d'Amboise and his emblem of burning rocks (*chaud mont*). Above are the arms of the Cardinal d'Amboise (with the Cardinal's hat), while over the entrance are the fleurs-de-lis of France and the monograms of Louis XII and Anne of Brittany.

In 1560 Chaumont was acquired by Catherine de Medici, with the sole view of forcing Diane de Poitiers to accept it in exchange for Chenonceau. Chaumont subsequently belonged to Henri de la Tour d'Auvergne, father of the Grand Turenne, the famous 17th-century commander and marshal of France; and under Henri IV to the Italian banker Scipion Sardini. In 1739 Nicolas Bertin de Vaugien bought the property and opened up the courtyard to the Loire, as at Ussé, by demolishing the north wing. Ten years later Jacques-Donatien Le Ray purchased the estate and in 1770 opened a pottery and glassworks in the outbuildings attracting artists such as the English master glass-painter Robert Scott Godfrey. Between 1772 and 1786 the Italian sculptor J. B. Nini, who specialized in terracotta portrait medallions, worked here.

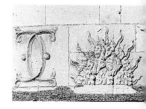

Chaumont: part of the frieze on one of the entrance towers.

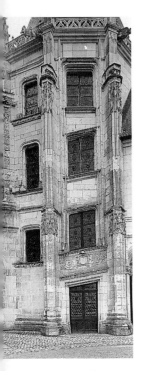

Chaumont: the octagonal staircase in the courtyard.

In the early 19th century Chaumont was left empty and decaying until about 1833 when it was acquired by the Comte d'Aramon, who began the work of restoration. Following his death in 1847 his widow married the Vicomte de Walsh who entrusted the work to the architect Jules Potier de la Morandière. In 1875 Chaumont was purchased by an heiress, Marie-Charlotte-Constance Say, who that year married Prince Amedée de Broglie (1849–1917). From 1878 the restoration was taken up by the architect Paul-Ernest Sanson (1838–1918), who designed numerous grand private houses in Paris in the decades around 1900. The Broglies lived at Chaumont in grand style, entertaining princes and maharajas until, in 1938, the Princesse sold Chaumont to the state.

Old photographs on display in the house, and reproduced in a small guide by Michel Melot and Jacqueline Melet-Sanson, convey the extent of restoration work. In the courtyard the rich octagonal staircase (a Gothic version of that at Blois) had been cut off at first floor level—the top is entirely reconstructed. The rich second-floor balcony on the east wing of the courtyard is wholly a creation of Sanson, with its rich mixture of Gothic and Renaissance detail. In doing this he took away the stone balconies to the first-floor windows and introduced Flamboyant lucarnes above. The aim was doubtless to create greater interest and richness at the top of the building in the manner of the illustration in *Les Très Riches Heures du Duc de Berry*.

The ground-floor rooms are mainly Sanson's: the dining-room has a particularly rich Gothic chimneypiece with three openings and the door linked in to the composition. The central newel of the main staircase has shell-headed niches, but otherwise the detail remains Gothic.

Upstairs the large **Council Chamber** hung with Brussels tapestry has a floor of 17th-century majolica tiles portraying a stag hunt, brought from a palace in Palermo by the Broglies, and is complete with built-in wall seats awaiting the councillors. At the end, in the so-called **Astrologer's Room**, is a 16th-century hooded fireplace with its original faded 16th-century colouring. The 1500

70

chapel was substantially restored at the end of the century.

Not to be missed are Sanson's original and lavishly equipped stables and harness room with distinctive overhanging roofs and dormers. A ménage for ponies was installed in the mushroom-shaped building known as the old dovecot.

The wide verdant park in which the château is set is largely a creation of the late 19th century. Félibien, towards 1700, describes Chaumont as 'having neither gardens nor park', adding that 'on the south side where there is countryside, it would be possible to lay out avenues and gardens as large as one might wish for'. In the event the Princesse Amedée de Broglie and the leading landscape architect Achille Duchêne created an English-style park, with informal planting and serpentine rides. Like almost all English parks on the continent the grass, however, is cut rather than grazed. Quite a number of the fine specimen trees, now in full maturity, including the cedars by the castle, were planted earlier in the century by the Comte d'Aramon.

CHENONCEAU

The view of Chenonceau reflected in the limpid waters of the Cher is almost as famous as that of the Taj Mahal. But who would guess that its origins lay in an ancient watermill on the river bank?

Perhaps the friendliest advice one can give on Chenonceau is don't go: too many people already do. It is open every day of the year, including Christmas Day, and boasts of being the most popular of all Loire châteaux. Looking at the endless throng of people walking up the smart avenue lined with white wooden tubs, who would dispute it? So if you do go, try to choose a time of day when the crowd is less intense.

The fief of Chenonceau was held by the Marques family from 1230. In 1411, after Jean Marques joined the Burgundy party, the château was razed. His son, Jean II Marques, however, was allowed in 1432 to reconstruct the château—his *donjon* survives on the first square moated island.

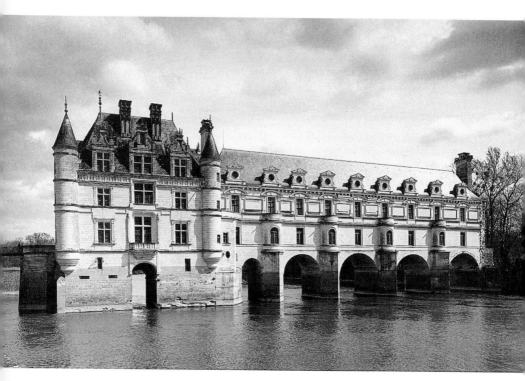

The château of Chenonceau spans the River Cher.

In 1513 the financier Thomas Bohier, receiver-general of the finances in Normandy, completed the purchase of the estate. Bohier was in Italy with Charles VIII, Louis XII and François I, and was appointed to administer the revenues of the Duchy of Milan. It appears likely, in view of Bohier's absence, that the work (as at Azay) was entrusted to his wife, the heiress Catherine Briçonnet.

On the foundations of the old mill in the river, he began in 1515 a new château, symmetrical in plan, which, with its round turrets prefigures Chambord, which was begun four year later. Chenonceau is on a square plan, like Chambord, and is symmetrical on the main axis with a broad gallery running from the entrance through the centre of the building, like the *portego* or first-floor hall of a Venetian palace, with a staircase opening off half-way along one side. Intriguingly Bohier was at this time in direct negotiation with Andrea Gritti the future Doge, though there is no evidence that he ever went to Venice.

However, in 1516 the Venetian architect Fra Giocondo was at Amboise and there is also a resemblance to the first model for Chambord made by Domenico da Cortona.

Externally, Chenonceau has the typical early Renaissance arrangement of vertically linked windows flanked by pilasters alternating with areas of plain wall and large elaborate dormers. The same style is found at the contemporary châteaux of Azay and Bury. Note the pilasters flanking the main doorway, inset with characteristic roundels. These carry powerful, richly carved semicircular balconies, corbelled out like the turrets on the corners of late medieval châteaux.

Bohier's estate became embroiled in the same complex of financial scandals as those of Berthelot at Azay-le-Rideau and Hurault at Cheverny and in 1435 the estate was ceded to the King. Henri II, who succeeded in 1547, gave Chenonceau to Diane de Poitiers, to the disgust of the Queen, Catherine de Medici, who questioned whether the royal estate could be alienated in this way. An elaborate charade was mounted by which ownership reverted briefly to Bohier in order to establish Diane's title.

Diane de Poitiers made two main contributions to Chenonceau; the creation of the large, moated walled garden on the left of the approach and the construction of the bridge across the Cher—though not the buildings on it. The château and garden of this time are beautifully recorded in a bird's-eye view by du Cerceau.

The raked walls of the new garden give it the look of contemporary military fortifications; the accounts show that an earth wall was held together by a wooden frame, faced with stone, and surrounded by water. Construction began in the spring of 1551 and continued until the winter of 1554. Du Cerceau's view shows the garden divided by *allées* into four rectangles, each subdivided by paths into six squares. Two hundred fruit trees were delivered from the garden of the Archbishop of Tours at Saint Averton by boat. It is not known what type of fruit these were, but later plum, cherry and pear trees were bought. Further elaborate gardens are shown on the south bank of the Cher. In 1556–57 Philibert de l'Orme, best known for his

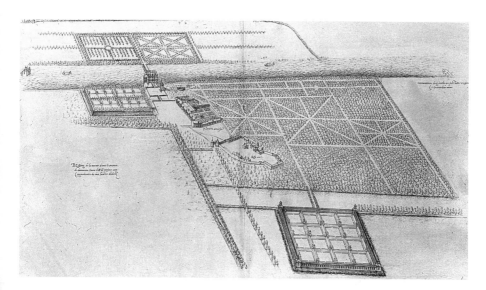

Chenonceau: bird's-eye view of the château and gardens by du Cerceau.

work on Diane de Poitiers' great château at Anet, built the bridge across the river. Following Henri II's death in 1559, Catherine de Medici, now Queen Mother, forced Diane de Poitiers to exchange Chenonceau for Chaumont.

Catherine held three spectacular garden displays at Chenonceau in 1560, 1563 and 1577, foreshadowing the great outdoor entertainments at Versailles a century later. The first of these was in March 1560 for the young François II and his queen, Mary Stuart, later to be better known as Mary Queen of Scots. A vast triumphal arch swathed with ivy swags stood over the drive. As the royal party passed by, trees burst into cascades of fireworks and fountains gushed with wine. The later fêtes were more licentious; in 1573 women dressed as men and Henri III and his acolytes were gorgeously dressed as girls.

Catherine de Medici added the galleries over the bridge in 1570–76. These are almost certainly the work of Jean Bullant, who was appointed as her architect in 1570. Bullants's mannerism is evident in the way the pediments of the upper-floor windows extend out over the intervening panels, which adds an element of complexity and ambiguity that contrasts with the simple rhythms of the early Renaissance façades. This play on shapes is taken up in the dormers with their bulbous sides and *œil-de-bœuf* windows. It was also, presumably, Bullant who drew up plans (engraved by du Cerceau) for a *cour d'honneur* enclosed by half-moon arcades, and a vast trapezoidal *avant-cour*. Nothing came of these, though the outbuildings on the approach follow the intended diagonal line.

Her widowed daughter-in-law, Louise de Lorraine, inherited the château in 1590, living out the life of a recluse. After her death Chenonceau was left to decay until, in 1730, it was acquired by one of the rising class of *fermier-général* (tax gatherer), Dupin. The story is told of the *curé* at Chenonceau who, at the Revolution, prevented the destruction of the château by pointing out it was the 'only bridge between Montricard and Bléré'. On the death of Mme Dupin's nephew, the Comte de Villeneuve, in 1863, Chenonceau was acquired by Madame Pelouze, who commissioned the architect Felix Roguet to restore the château to its appearance in du Cerceau's engravings. Happily he stopped short of demolishing Bullant's galleries across the river. A great deal of stonework was renewed, and, as a result, Chenonceau lacks the patina one hopes to find in a building of this age. Early photographs show elaborate lead cresting on the main ridges of the roofs, which has since disappeared, perhaps during the shelling by the Germans in 1940 or during the Allied bombing of 1944. More recently the elaborate finials have been replaced in resin.

Given the number of visitors it is inevitable, as at Azay, that the interiors are somewhat empty and impersonal. Architecturally the most intriguing element is the maverick vaulted hall of Renaissance date with bosses set wilfully out of line, and the complex vaulting of the staircase. Some of the rooms have rich elements of 19th-century decor.

The galleries over the river are unexpectedly plain, apart from the vast, truly astonishing chimneypieces suggesting the hand of Bullant, and of similar size and character as one at the Château of Écouen north of Paris.

Recently, the bedroom of Louise de Lorraine at the top of the house, has been recreated following contemporary descriptions. After the assassination of Henri III at

Saint-Cloud in 1589 she had shut herself away in proud and theatrical mourning. Now the room has been entirely repainted in black, with giant silver tears on the walls, and a bed in black velvet and taffeta, with white silk fringes and crowns of thorns.

LE CHESNAY

Though not in any guidebook I have seen, this house is worth a small detour for anyone driving south from Orléans into the Sologne. Here, in pretty, well wooded, countryside, you suddenly pass first one, then a second, stupendous avenue of giant firs in full maturity.

You emerge at a rural *rond-point* with farm buildings in two corners; in front is the château, preceded by a long, narrow garden, postponing the moment of arrival still further. The house itself (built early this century) is more like a fanciful seaside villa than a château, with roofs like the hats you would expect in a production of *Madame Butterfly*.

Le Chesnay is south-east of Vouzon on the D 129. Take

Le Chesnay.

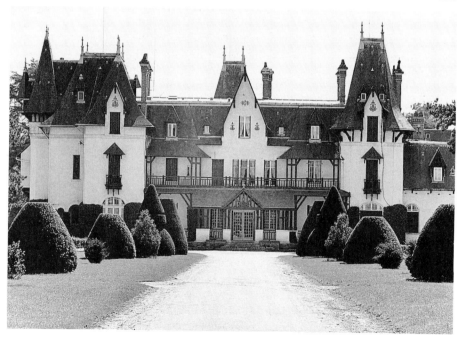

the N 20 south from Orléans and turn off left 9.5 km (6 miles) after La Ferté-Saint-Aubin on the D 153 to Vouzon.

For those tiring of vast, barely furnished rooms, Cheverny is cast in a different mould. Here is an artistocratic house, immaculately maintained by its traditional owners, and invariably photographed with the Cheverny hounds and huntsmen striding out across the lawns.

Cheverny was first opened to the public after the First World War by the Marquis de Vibraye, who left it to his nephew the Vicomte de Sigalas, and today it ranks equally as a tourist attraction with Azay, Chambord and Chenonceau.

There was an early 16th-century château here, described in the archives as complete with 'moats, chain drawbridge, gunloops, turrets and barbicans' built for Raoul Hurault, Minister of Finances for François I. Cheverny was elevated to a *vicomté* in 1577 and a *comté* (the equivalent of an English earldom) in 1582. In 1625 Henri Hurault, governor and bailiff of Blois, embarked on a complete reconstruction, in which contrary to the usual practice, all trace and even memory of the earlier château were obliterated.

Félibien, writing in 1681 in his *Memoires pour servir à l'histoire des maisons royales* says, 'One Boyer of Blois was the architect'. This is Jacques Bougier, master mason, who was also involved at the château of Blois. He died in

CHEVERNY

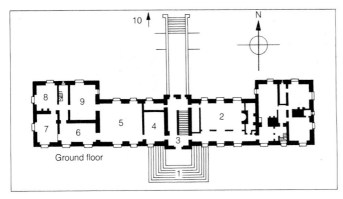

Cheverny
1. Main entrance
2. Dining-room
3. Staircase
4. Antechamber
5. Grand salon
6. Vestibule
7. Petit salon
8. Library
9. Tapestry room
10. To the orangery

Ground floor

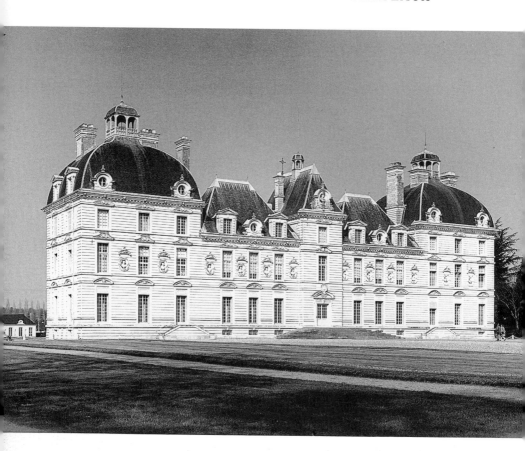

Cheverny: the 17th-century château.

1632, but the building work was largely completed two years later.

Approaching the entrance front you have the impression the house is constructed of crisp white painted wood. What you see, however, is not clapboard, but continuously chanelled stonework that is almost neo-classical in its precision. What one would expect of a Louis XIII building is red brick and stone (as at La Ferté-Saint-Aubin), and this is precisely what you find on the garden front at Cheverny.

What appeals about the entrance front is the exact precison of the horizontals—like lines drawn with a ruler. The same crisp geometry marks the steps leading up to the front door. Typically 17th-century is the play on the pediments (as at contemporary Brissac), different for each storey. Particularly elegant are the swan pediments like those on early 18th-century bureau bookcases. The niches between also have scrolled pediments capped by shells.

The criticism has often been made that the end pavilions, with their squared domes, overwhelm the narrow centre; the explanation is that, as at Azay and Serrant, the central block is entirely filled with a tunnel-vaulted stair. Here—a century later—arches are introduced between the parallel arms producing exciting cross vistas. On the stair are the initials 'F L 1634'. Whether this refers to Bougier's successor or the author of the crisp decorative carving is not clear.

Cheverny has a very fine set of interiors with the elaborate painted *boiseries* and chimneypieces typical of the second quarter of the 17th century. This painted decoration can be attributed convincingly to Jean Mosnier. However it is overlaid with a considerable amount of rather good 19th-century restoration and repainting. This is most obvious in the dining-room to the right of the entrance, with its voluptuous built-in sideboard and corridor which were added on one side.

Cheverny: the entrance.

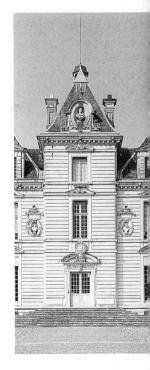

The **Salle des Gardes**, or Armoury, on the first floor is lit, like all the main rooms, by windows on both sides, showing the typical single-pile (one room deep) plan of the Louis XIII period. The painting by Mosnier over the fireplace represents *The Death of Adonis*. The wainscot is painted with a series of allegorical scenes taken from contemporary emblematic books, with proverbial tags like 'self-love was my downfall'.

On the first floor you can also visit the private apartments, recently decorated in exactly the manner of the bedrooms in a grand English country house—though for all the *confort anglais* the furniture is obviously French. Also on the first floor the **King's Bedchamber** has a particularly fine 17th-century panelled ceiling by Mosnier, with friezes of *putti* painted on a gold ground. The central panel portrays Perseus and Andromeda.

The **Trophy Room** behind the stables has almost as many antlers as in certain Edwardian shooting lodges in the Scottish highlands.

CHINON

Chinon's place in history is secure. It was here in 1429 that the Maid of Orléans, Joan of Arc, at last gained her audience with the Dauphin which led 20 years later to the dramatic expulsion of the English from France. (Following Henry V's victory at Agincourt in 1415, England's possessions in France had reached almost their greatest extent, embracing Paris itself.) Yet in one sense Chinon is predominantly an English castle and it is sad that the remains are almost as fragmentary as those at Richard Coeur de Lions's great castle of Château Gaillard in Normandy.

The site was occupied in prehistoric times; a Roman *castrum* was built on the rocky spur on which the castle stands. It is a natural redoubt, protected by a high cliff to the south and steep gullies to the north and west. The first château was constructed in the second half of the tenth century by the Count of Blois, Thibaud le Tricheur, and in 1044 it passed to the house of Anjou.

Major works were carried out by Henry II of England, the first of the house of Anjou to wear the English crown. Henry's prodigious activity as a castle builder was noted by the Abbot of Mont-Saint-Michel, Robert of Torigni.

The huge fortress of Chinon stands on a commanding site with the town and river below.

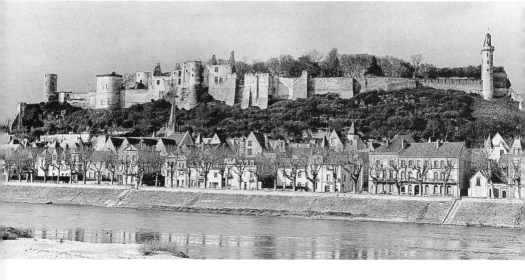

80

Not only in Normandy, but also in England, in the Duchy of Aquitaine, in the County of Anjou, in Maine and Touraine, he either repaired old castles and palaces or built new ones.

According to the *History of the King's Works*, the authoritative source on English royal buildings, the grand total of expenditure upon castle works, as recorded in the Pipe Rolls alone, was just over £46,000, or an average of £780 a year, at a time when the basic revenue of the Crown was less than £10,000 a year. In England Henry II spent heavily on defending the south-east coast, and the Scottish and Welsh marches. The significance of Chinon was that it lay in the centre of his French possessions.

In 1205 Chinon fell after a seige of a year to the French; subsequently Philippe Auguste, Saint Louis and Philip III all made frequent visits. From 1449 Charles VII made the castle the permanent seat of his court, installing his favourite Agnes Sorel in a small house, Le Roberdeau, outside the walls. The later Valois kings, however, abandoned the château, and during the Wars of Religion it was occupied several times by the Protestants. In the 17th century the Dukes of Richelieu went a stage further in demolishing parts of the building including Charles VI's *grande salle*.

Further damage was done in the Revolution, but in 1840 it was classified a Monument Historique, and in 1854 saved by the intervention of Prosper Mérimée, romantic novelist and father of preservation in France.

Today the château impresses above all by its spectacular site above the town and river, and the fine views it commands over fertile countryside which provides an excellent light red wine. In architectural terms it consists of three medieval fortresses, aligned east to west, and separated by deep ditches, the **Fort Saint-Georges**, the **Château du Milieu**, and the **Château du Coudray**. The last two date back to the years around 1100. Henry II constructed the Fort Saint-Georges on a rectangular plan to protect the eastern approach and at the south-west corner built the **Tour du Moulin**. Apart from the walls and various towers, the principal survival is the shell of the **Royal Lodgings**, overlooking the Vienne.

COMBREUX

The 19th-century château is worth no more than a small detour: its charm is that the whole layout can easily be appreciated from the passing road. It was built in an idiosyncratic Gothic style around a medieval core, by the Duc de la Rochefoucauld d'Estissac, and stands in a moat that is but a few yards from the Orléans canal. The most distinctive feature is the freestanding tower in the courtyard, with tapering buttresses that give it the look of a rocket. At the upper end of the grounds the *communs* are built facing the château.

Combreux.

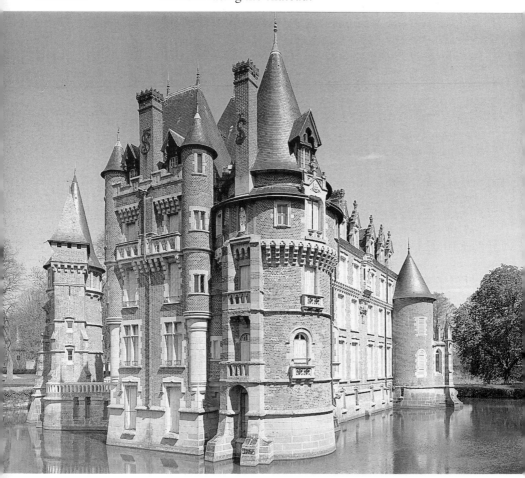

Combreux is just north of the village of the same name along the D 9. Take the N 60 from Orléans and at Châteauneuf-sur-Loire turn left onto the D 10 for Vitry-aux-Loges and, shortly before, turn right onto the D 9 for Combreux.

LE COUDRAY-MONTPENSIER

The silhouette of the château stands out prominently amidst the open rolling landscape south of Chinon, and is best seen after a sudden shower when its slate roofs glisten against a dark sky and its white walls are bathed in a shaft of sun. The property is encircled by a long park wall, with trees behind, and is a reminder of what, in the Loire, it is all too easy to forget: not every château is preserved principally for the benefit of tourists. Le Coudray-Montpensier, as numerous buildings in the grounds announce, is a centre for handicapped children.

The château's romance lies in its unusual plan—not a rectangle like so many, but a near circle, punctuated by massive machicolated towers, with the slate roofs sitting right on top of the battlements. On one side the circuit of walls is broken leaving the courtyard open to view.

The château was built in stages between the late 14th and late 15th centuries, by successive owners—Louis de France, Duc d'Anjou, who bought the property in 1380 and died four years later; his widow Marie de Blois, who died in 1404 (the low wing in the courtyard has an M and the arms of France); Pierre de Bournan and his widow, and their son Louis. The name of Montpensier was added in 1481 by Louis de Bourbon.

The château is surrounded by a dry moat and overlooks terraced gardens now largely growing wild. This garden, it seems, is a restoration laid out by Henri Lafargue and Albert Laprade for the aviator Pierre Latécoère in 1930.

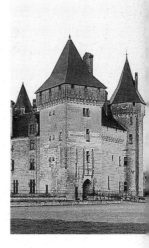

The entrance of Le Coudray-Montpensier.

LA FERTÉ-IMBAULT

The gates of La Ferté-Imbault are firmly closed, but the view of it from the road at the east end of the village is so splendid that, at the least, it is worth a detour.

A château, built here in 980 for Humbault, seigneur of Vierzon, was reduced to ruins by the English in 1356. In

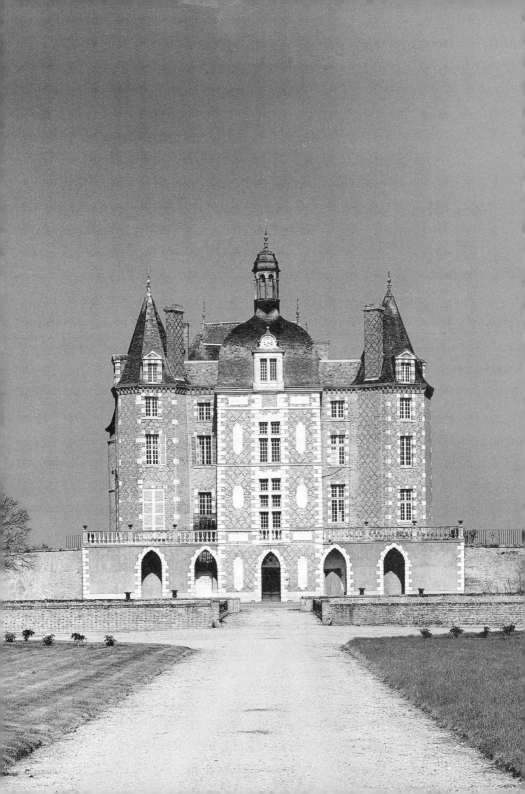

1450 it was acquired by Robert II d'Etampes and reconstructed by his grandson Jean, soon after his marriage in 1499. This building was destroyed in turn by the Protestants and reconstructed from 1627 onwards by Jacques d'Etampes.

Here is a classic example of the way farm and stable buildings laid out symmetrically on either side of the approach can be used to add grandeur and formality to a composition. The buildings of the farm court are of plain red brick. A broad bridge leading across a dry moat leads to an inner courtyard flanked by more symmetrical outbuildings.

The château itself stands on a balustraded platform approached by steps within one of the arches below. The square plan with corner towers has distant echoes of Chambord; curiously the octagonal corner towers are slightly skewed. The centre is emphasized by a projecting square tower with a curving roof *à l'impériale* like the one on the near contemporary front at Brissac—it is complete with the open cupola which at Brissac has vanished.

The château is constructed of the red brick that is typical of the Sologne with a scattering of stone dressings emphasizing the corners and windows. The centre is emphasized by more extensive use of stonework and the introduction of bold lozenge-shaped panels. Note how the diapering extends to the tall chimneys. Also remarkable, but only barely visible, are the succession of garden terraces on which the house stands.

(Opposite) The 17th-century château of La Ferté-Imbault.

Architecturally this splendid château has one serious flaw easily concealed in photographs: the two halves of the *corps-de-logis* do not match. Yet the present owner's affection and enthusiasm for the house is so intense that it is impossible not to come away enchanted.

The delight of many 17th-century houses lies in the grandeur and formality of the *communs*. La Ferté stands at right angles to the main road south from Orléans, at the entrance to the town, and the château is set on a large rectangular platform in the middle of a broad moat. The pediment of the entrance arch is sliced through to provide

LA FERTÉ-SAINT-AUBIN

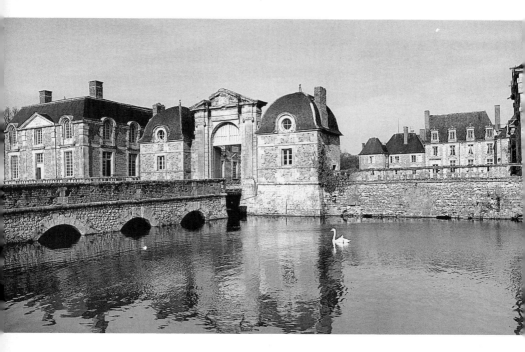

La Ferté-Saint-Aubin seen from across the moat.

recesses for the levers of a drawbridge (an unexpected feature at this date) and flanked by a pair of gate lodges with roofs like deerstalker hats. All the buildings are in the characteristic Louis XIII mixture of mellow red brick with stone trim. The long freestanding wings contained the stables and other offices.

There is mention of a *château fort* here in the 12th century. The present building was begun by Henri de Saint-Nectaire, for whom La Ferté was raised to a marquessate in 1617. He built the *'petit château'*, the small left half of the *corps-de-logis*. His son Henri II was a Marshal of France and for him La Ferté was raised to a duchy. He built the major part of the *corps-de-logis*, perhaps continuing to live in the old house while it was under construction. He never completed the rebuilding so the two halves of the *corps-de-logis* stand lop-sided.

The design is attributed to the architect Théodore II Lefèvre, known as Lefèvre d'Orléans, who supplied the design for the Parisian *hôtel* of Sennecterres, demolished at the end of the 17th century to make way for the Place des Victoires. The two long freestanding wings were conceived at the same time, but probably not finished till later; the wing on the left is sometimes dated 1728.

A plan in the 18th-century *Atlas Trudaine* shows the extent of the network of canals around the château fed by the adjacent river Cosson. This is a typical, if quite plain example of a French formal garden of the baroque period. On the island behind the moat, in place of the 17th-century *parterres*, stands a large neo-Gothic chapel.

In 1746 the estate was acquired by the Comte de Lowendahl and later, in 1822, by the Prince d'Essling. None of these, it seems, had the money or the inclination to complete the *corps-de-logis* though at some point an attempt had been made to bring harmony by introducing matching windows to the earlier wing.

When M. Guyot, the present owner, acquired La Ferté, the right-hand wing was a shell. It has now been re-roofed and is let for conferences and receptions. In the stables on the left he has introduced 17th-century stalls, which, ironically, were thrown out of the Château de Dampierre in the Île de France to make a tea-room.

Within three months of purchasing La Ferté, M. Guyot had opened and furnished 23 rooms. This is a rare French château where you can explore every interior from cellar to attic and find out where all the secret doors in the panelling lead to. For him there is no castaway object, however humble, that is not a candidate for putting on show. Even a discarded section of *parquet à la française* is put out so that you can examine its construction. Beneath the eaves is a fascinating collection of carpentry tools and patent roof tiles made in the village in the last century.

Many Loire châteaux, particularly the earlier ones, were substantially restored in the 19th century. Fougères escaped such attentions because from 1814 until the end of the century it housed a spinning mill, and thereafter was home to the poor and needy. By 1932 it had so deteriorated that the state moved in to acquire it.

Over the last half century repairs have been carried out carefully and conservatively and a comparison with

FOUGÈRES-SUR-BIÈVRE

A view of the courtyard in the 15th-century château of Fougères-sur-Bièvre, which has survived almost completely unchanged.

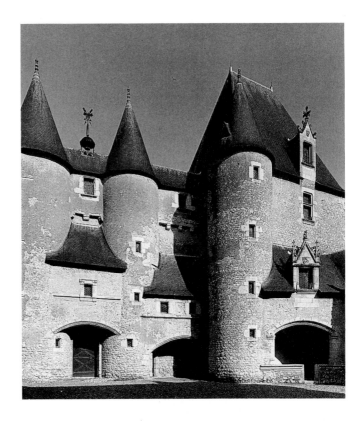

photographs taken around 1900 shows very few changes apart from the replacement of casement windows by leaded lights.

An earlier château had been destroyed by the English in the Hundred Years War. Pierre de Refuge, whose financial skills were exercised first for the Duc d'Orléans, then Charles VIII and Louis XI, obtained from Louis XI (before the King's death in 1483) authorization to '*rétablir le château de Fougères en château-fort*'. Pierre died in 1497, leaving Fougères to his grandson and it remained in the family until the end of the 17th century.

The château stands in the centre of the village, its moats long since filled in. It is built on a quadrangular plan with a square tower at the north corner. It is sometimes said that this is part of the *donjon* of an earlier château, but its detail matches the rest of the building and the walls are

88

very thin. Work continued after the death of Pierre de Refuge under the direction of his son-in-law, Jean de Villebresmes. Inside the courtyard there is an arcade, a parallel to the one at Blois. The chapel inside the château retains few features, but the gallery is interesting.

Take D 956 south from Blois towards Contres. After about 15 km (9 miles) turn right on the D 52 for Fougères.

Like Amboise, Blois and Saumur, Gien dominates a town on the banks of the Loire, and like them it was, in effect, a royal domain. It was built for Anne de France, daughter of Louis XI, wife of Pierre II de Bourbon, who had been charged with the regency during the minority of her brother Charles VIII (1483–98). The present château, on the site of an earlier one, was built in 1494–1500, and is similar in style to the Louis XII wing at Blois begun in 1498. It is in red brick with extensive criss-cross diapering in black brick, without a trace of Renaissance detail.

Following extensive damage during bombardments in 1940 and 1944, which substantially destroyed the town, the château has been restored and opened as a **Musée de la Chasse**. The museum contains an exceptionally rich, varied and well-displayed collection of arms and trophies and every kind of decorative art associated with hunting—paintings, prints, bronzes, porcelain and wallpapers.

GIEN

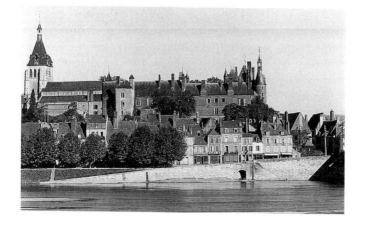

Gien: the château (c. 1494–1500) viewed from across the Loire.

Architecturally, there is relatively little of interest, though the great hall at the top with an open timber roof is impressive with the curious effect of one fireplace set above another, where floors have been removed.

In a lobby near the entrance are 19th-century prints from the *Encyclopédie d'Architecture* by the architect Just Lisch; these show plans for an early restoration of the château as a *sous-préfecture* and tribunal that were only partially carried out.

Be sure to look into the remarkable church, next to the château, reconstructed in 1950–54 by Paul Gélis, architecte en chef des Monuments Historiques, a vision of Byzantium regained with strong influences of Hagia Sophia. Of the original 15th-century church only the clock tower remains.

GUÉ-PÉAN

Gué-Péan is tucked away in the woods, 24 km (15 miles) east of Chenonceau, 24 km south-west of Cheverny, looking out over a pleasant flat-bottomed vale. Architecturally it is at once imposing and irregular, and as the proprietor now lets rooms it is relatively easy to see.

The builder of the house must have been François Alamand, controller-general of the *gabelles* (the hated salt tax), who died in 1550. The two towers on the entrance side may be the work of his father, but the Renaissance detail to the windows suggests the 1540s or thereabouts. This corresponds with the elevation of the *seigneurie* into the higher dignity of the *châtellenie* in 1543 by François I.

The château is dominated by a massive circular tower with a bell-shaped dome, even more pronounced in silhouette than those at Valençay. But though the corner towers are irregular and treated quite differently, the plan is a regular quadrangle. The entrance is flanked by flat-topped *demilune* bastions looking like artillery platforms, but the rest of the defences are more for show, though there are gunloops at the foot of the walls. The machicolations of the bell-topped tower, for example, are inset with Renaissance shells. Most curious of all is the actual site of the house, for though it commands the ground to the north, massive excavations have had to be

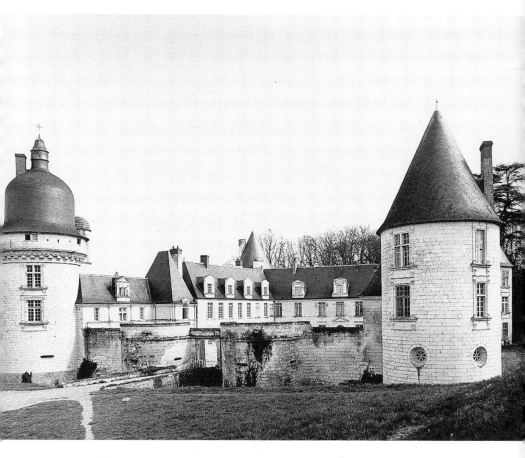

made on two sides to provide breathing space for the windows.

Inside the courtyard are two matching Renaissance pavilions, on an L-shaped plan with the characteristic motif of a large column below and a much smaller one above. This formula of large widely-spaced columns below and shorter, more frequent columns above is found in early Renaissance courtyards in Italy. On the ground floor are arcaded loggias paved in stone. In the corner of that on the right, under a squinch, is a handsome panelled door into the chapel. The remaining façades in the courtyard are 17th-century; the wing on the right is topped by a flat, first-floor terrace.

Gué-Péan: the early 16th-century château.

HERBAULT

This is a striking small château given character by its steep roofs and conical towers. A bridge leads across to a broad *avant-cour* flanked by low ranges of *communs* or offices.

The *corps-de-logis* is in the form of an L, rather like Azay, and was built between 1520–25 for Nicolas Foyal, superintendent of works at Chambord. Originally there was a balancing wing on the right of the *cour d'honneur*, but this was demolished in the last century.

The château has three substantial towers on the exterior with smaller towers in the internal angles of the *cour d'honneur*. The walls have attractive diapered brickwork with stone dressings to the windows. The roof ridge and the tops of the towers are ornamented with a rich cresting and finials. The *communs*, which contain a remarkable chapel, were added in the first quarter of the 17th century for Raymond Phelypeaux, secretary of state, who acquired the estate in 1591.

Herbault: the corps-de-logis dates from 1520–25.

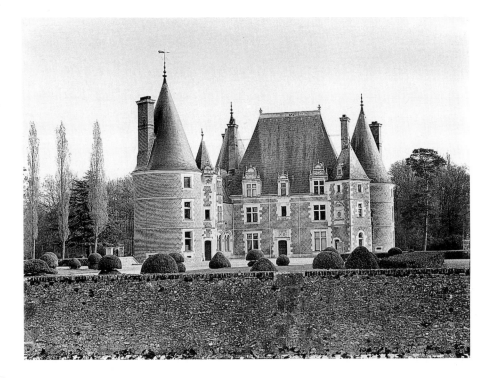

Langeais is the classic 15th-century fortress, proud, dominating and with a silhouette of conical towers that could only be French. For those who like to take photographs, or simply admire, it is worth not only looking back across the Loire, but climbing the streets behind the château to obtain a view over the rooftops.

From the entrance side the sheer muscularity of the circular towers is breathtaking. No longer are they punctuation marks rising above a lower wall; instead the whole wall is of even height and the wall-walk continues the whole length, emphasizing the curve of each tower. Langeais, however, also has a characteristically rich late medieval silhouette with an extra stage to each tower and numerous tall chimneys, proclaiming state rooms and comfortable living quarters within.

Langeais retains the ruins of the earliest Romanesque *donjon* to survive in France, begun in 994 for Fulk Nerra (the Black Falcon), the powerful and treacherous Count of Anjou, and the most fearsome feudal brigand of his age. Langeais was one of a ring of *donjons* with which he fortified the whole county of Anjou against the Counts of Blois, Chartres and Tours.

Langeais passed to the Kings of England, as heirs of Anjou, but was retaken—like so much—by Philippe Auguste from King John in 1206. During the Hundred Years War it constantly changed hands; in 1428 it was handed back to the French on condition that it was entirely razed except for the *'grosse tour'* or *donjon*.

The present château was built by command of Louis XI at the end of the promontory, about 100 m from the *donjon*. Jean Bourré (builder of Le Plessis-Bourré) directed the works. Jean Briçonnet, mayor of Tours, was charged to make the necessary payments between 1465 and 1467.

It was here that the famous marriage of Charles VIII and Anne of Brittany took place in 1491. Duchess Anne had first been married by proxy to Maximilian of Austria, the Holy Roman Emperor; after so much trouble with the English kings and their claims to the French throne, it was understandable that Charles VIII did not want another

Langeais: the château was built for Louis XI between 1465 and 1467.

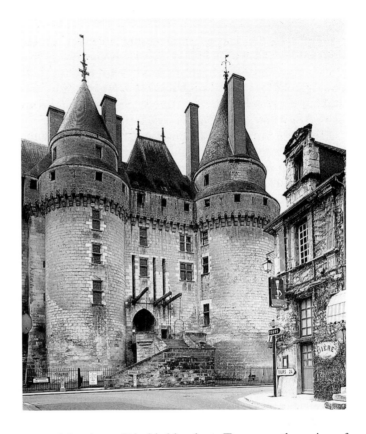

overmighty 'vassal' in his kingdom. To secure the union of France and Brittany the marriage contract stipulated that if the King died first without an heir, the queen was to marry his successor. This proved foresight indeed, for when Charles VIII cracked his head on a lintel at Amboise, Queen Anne married Louis XII.

Thereafter Langeais falls from the pages of history, changing hands but little altered until, in 1797, it was acquired by a burgher of Tours, Charles François Moisant, who left it to fall into ruin.

Then in 1839 it was acquired by a Parisian attorney, Christophe Baron, who started the reconstruction. In 1886 the château was acquired by Jacques Siegfried, who embarked on a more serious, indeed monumental, restoration, removing the more fanciful elements of his predecessor. His architect was Lucien Roy. Siegfried assembled a large collection of Flamboyant Gothic furniture, some original, some copies from authentic pieces, as well as numerous 15th- and 16th-century tapestries. Much attention was lavished on the floors and chimneypieces. But be warned there are numerous waxwork figures awaiting you in the rooms.

Siegfried left the château and all its contents to the Institut de France in 1904, and in the 1970s a formal garden was laid out to the design of Louis Hautecœur, the great historian of French classical architecture, on the model of Queen Anne's garden at Amboise.

LOCHES

The château of Loches is among the most remarkable medieval fortress enceintes surviving in France. Gregory of Tours mentions a fortress here in the 6th century; destroyed in 742, this was rebuilt by Charles the Bald. From 987 it was held by the Counts of Anjou, and came into the possession of the Angevin kings of England in 1193. It was seized for Philippe Auguste; the next year Richard Coeur de Lion freed it after a siege of three hours. After Richard's death Philippe Auguste retook the château, and gave it to the son of his victorious captain, Dreu de Mello. In 1249 Saint Louis brought Loches back directly under royal control. It served as an important residence for Charles VII and Louis XI. From the end of the 15th century to the Revolution it served as a prison which at least ensured its upkeep.

Fulk Nerra, Count of Anjou, began the mighty *donjon* as one of a series of strategic fortresses including Montbazon, Montrichard and Langeais, intended to consolidate his conquest of Touraine. Continued and strengthened after his death in 1040, the *donjon* still dominates the valley of the Indre. Built of rough stone, it is given a strongly vertical character by semi-circular buttresses added on three sides towards the end of the 11th century.

In the 12th century the English surrounded the *donjon* with a complex series of defensive enceintes. In the 13th century the enceinte was strengthened at the southern end

Loches: the château is one of the most remarkable medieval fortress enceintes in France.

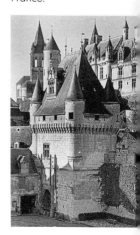

by three unusual towers of almond shape, projecting out like prows. In the 15th century the **Tour Neuve**, in effect a new *donjon*, was added. This contains three floors of lodgings (with fireplaces and *garderobes* over a basement with a hemispherical vault). Here Ludovico Sforza, Duke of Milan, was incarcerated while a prisoner of Louis XII between 1500 and 1508.

In the outer enceinte stand the fine Gothic collegiate church and the *logis du roi* composed of two buildings. The **Vieux Logis** dates from the 14th century, but is heavily restored particularly in the upper stages. It contains nonetheless some fine sculptural detail as well as the tomb of Agnès Sorel, mistress of Charles VII. The **Nouveau Logis**, dating from the late 15th and early 16th centuries (Charles VIII and Louis XII) is still Flamboyant Gothic in style, recalling the Louis XII wing at Blois, without the Italian detail. It contains the delightful **Oratory of Anne of Brittany** decorated with a profusion of the Queen's emblems—the ermine and the cords of St Francis.

LE LUDE

The entrance to the château is in a sleepy back street of the town; once through it you are confronted by the entrance front with its two massive cylindrical towers of medieval proportions, but Renaissance detail. The narrow *cour d'honneur* speaks an altogether different language, that of an aristocratic Parisian *hôtel*. Le Lude's architectural history is complicated, spanning hundreds of years, and by no means definitively charted.

A château was built here in the 10th century by the Counts of Anjou against the Normans. In 1457 this became the property of the Daillon family. Jean II de Daillon, chamberlain of Louis XI and governor of Dauphiné, began the present château. It is constructed on a square plan with massive cylindrical corner towers rising from a deep, broad, dry moat. Originally there was a *bassecour* to the east of the château but this was levelled in the 17th century for the present *parterre*; subterranean passages survive beneath. The north front to the left of the entrance retains, despite 19th-century restorations, its

(Opposite) Le Lude: the entrance courtyard of the Renaissance château.

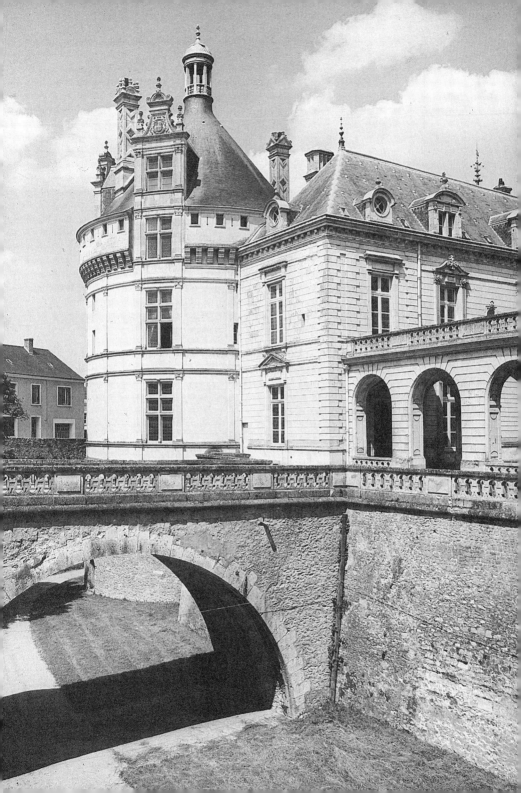

15th-century character, with Gothic dormers and a terrace carried on flattened arches. This is the work of Jacques Gendrot, clerk of the works to René d'Anjou.

Jean II de Daillon died in 1480, and building was continued by his son, Jacques de Daillon, chamberlain of both Louis XII and François I. The south front was evidently under construction in the lifetime of Louis XII as it has his porcupines on the balustrade—here carried on pure semicircular arches. Work continued during the 1520s until the death of Jacques de Daillon in 1532.

Stonework has evidently been renewed, but the detail is similar to Blois and Chambord with panelled pilasters framing the vertically linked windows and dormers crowned with shell pediments and candelabra. As in other Renaissance châteaux the machicolations and fortified wall-walk around the towers are retained, adorned with medallions and flowers.

Timoléon de Daillon, lived at Le Lude from 1619 until 1651 and it was presumably he who remodelled the internal courtyard—the channelled stonework is similar to that of Cheverny which dates from c.1625–35. Previously the courtyard had been open on the east towards the *bassecour*; now this arrangement was reversed. The grand terrace running for 180 m (200 yds) is his work (1642) and provides a spectacular panorama of the river and meadows beyond. The sundial at the end of the terrace bears his initials TMD, and those of his wife Marie Feydeau. For his son, Louis XIV elevated Le Lude into a dukedom in 1675.

After the death of the duke in 1685 the château was little used until the estate was purchased in 1751 by a Frenchman of Dutch extraction, M. du Valaer, a member of the *Compagnie des Indes*. His niece, the Marquise de Vieuville, inherited in 1785, and her husband commissioned the architect Jean Barré (who also worked at Montgeoffroy) to remodel the east front overlooking the garden. Barré brought the new front out almost flush with the towers; the design, though chastely Louis-Seize in its lack of ornament, in other ways looks back to the 17th century with its vertically linked windows and pavilion roofs.

During the 19th century extensive restoration was carried out for the Talhouët family who inherited the château. The initials TR on the chimneys stand for the Marquis René de Talhouët-Roy. This restoration included the rebuilding of the **Tour du Diable** at the north-west corner, which was originally much smaller, to the same proportions as the south-west tower.

Inside, the most important Renaissance survival are the wall paintings in the *cabinet* in the south-east tower, discovered in 1853, hidden under whitewash, by the architect Delarue. It is thought that these may have been concealed at the time of the Revolution, when anything heraldic was at risk. The paintings are dated from between 1559 and 1585 and have been attributed to Giovanni da Udine, one of Raphael's collaborators. However Dominique Bozo has shown that they are inspired by illustrations to the *Triumph of Petrarch* (*c*.1515) in a manuscript which belonged to Jacques de Daillon and by an engraving in a volume entitled *Les Quadrins Historiques de la Bible*, published in 1553. The walls are divided into large painted scenes (look out for Noah's ark), and scenes from the life of Joseph in arches under the vaults.

In the middle of the east wing is the oval **Grand Salon**, by Barré, painted in the characteristic pearl grey of the late 18th century. Further remodelling was carried out in the 19th century, notably the vaulted staircase and the elaborate vestibule with a shallow coffered vault similar to those opening off the central staircase at Chambord. The dining-room has a massive stone chimneypiece with the emblems of François I (the salamander) and his wife Claude (the ermine).

The château, which originally bore the name of Maillé, occupies a commanding position above the Loire. A first château, of uncertain date, was destroyed in 1096 and rebuilt by Hardouin de Maillé. The present building appears to date back to the first half of the 13th century. It is laid out on a regular quadrilateral plan with circular towers at the corners and the centres of each face, save to the south where the slope alone is sufficient for defence.

LUYNES

Luynes: the château is on a quadrangular plan and dates back to the first half of the 13th century.

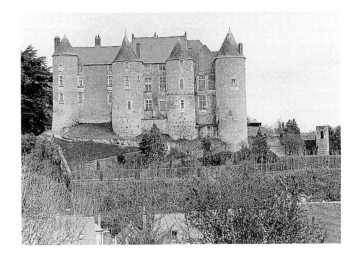

The *donjon*, described in 1634 as a *'forte grosse et haute tour'*, disappeared soon after that date.

During the reign of Louis XI, windows were opened in the towers and courtyards by Hardouin IX de Maillé. On the west side of the courtyard he built an elegant *logis* in brick and stone with an octagonal staircase tower. From this springs, at second-floor level, a bartisan, or projecting turret, in which the stair continues. This was extensively restored in the 19th century.

In 1619 Maillé was bought by Charles d'Albert, seigneur de Luynes, who that year became a duke and renamed Maillé after his new dukedom. Charles d'Albert had been a page to Louis XIII before he became king; together in 1617 they plotted the assassination of Marie de Medici's favourite, Concini.

The new duke built a range of apartments across the south terrace, but of this only the western portion survives. It is built in the same grey stone as the medieval towers.

MÉNARS

Note: Ménars was open to the public for many years, but has recently changed hands and at the time of writing is closed for restoration. Check before setting out.

The association with Madame de Pompadour, who

acquired the château in 1760, just four years before her death, suggests that Ménars will be a Trianon or *pavillon de plaisir*, and photographs taken from across the Loire reinforce the impression of quite a modest building. But the breadth of the river deceives the eye and the scale of Ménars is in fact positively ducal.

You catch a glimpse of the huge *communs* coming from the direction of Blois; as you turn into the axial approach the formality is overpowering, with double rows of neatly clipped trees leading to high iron railings and gates set between two widely spaced lodges.

The present *corps-de-logis* was built for Guillaume Cuarron about 1646. As Conseiller du Roi and Trésorier Général de l'Extraordinaire des Guerres, he benefitted from lucrative war contracts. This building is constructed in the characteristic Louis XIII manner of red brick with stone dressings.

On his death, his son Jean-Jacques, brother-in-law of

Ménars seen from across the Loire. The *corps-de-logis* dates from c. 1646. The wings were added by Madame de Pompadour who acquired Ménars in 1760.

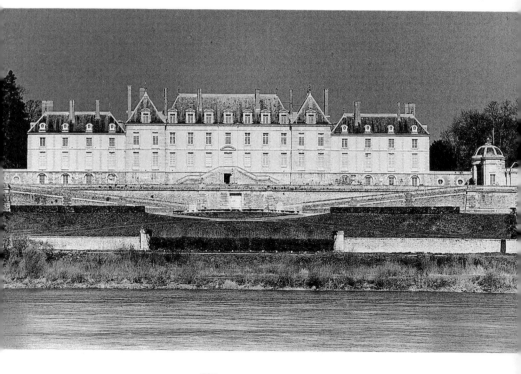

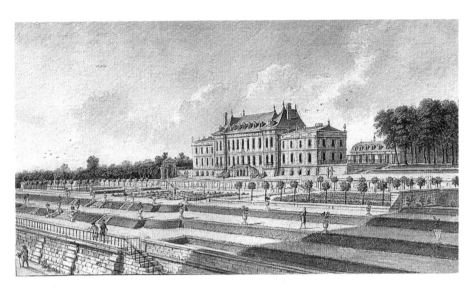

Ménars: the mid-18th-century gardens designed for Madame de Pompadour.

Louis XIV's brilliant finance minister Colbert, greatly enlarged the estate which was elevated to a marquessate in 1676. Jean-Jacques laid out the park with *parterres*, a bowling-green, canal and *pièces d'eau*.

Madame de Pompadour on acquiring the château commissioned Ange-Jacques Gabriel, architect of the Petit Trianon, to enlarge the house. Gabriel's wings with their original low roofs are shown in the drawing.

In 1765 the property passed to Madame de Pompadour's brother the Marquis de Marigny, *directeur des bâtiments du Roi*. He commissioned the leading neo-classical architect Jacques Soufflot (designer of the Panthéon in Paris) to design a new single-storey entrance range at the front of the *corps-de-logis*, while on the garden front he constructed a rotunda attached to the orangery and linked to the château by an underground staircase. With its columns imprisoned in blocked stonework, this is an example of the new 'elemental' architecture pioneered by Ledoux, Boullée and Soufflot. Here Marigny assembled a remarkable collection of sculpture consisting of monumental vases, busts and mythological statues, now largely dispersed except for a few pieces built into the symmetrical terraces which extend right to the Loire—these were also designed by Marigny.

To the east, Marigny, inspired by Chambers at Kew, wanted a pagoda, only to be told stuffily by Soufflot that a director of the *bâtiments du Roi* 'could not build in either the Chinese or Arab taste'. Marigny took no notice and commissioned a design from de Wailly instead, but alas the pagoda no longer exists.

Inside, Soufflot's three rooms were opened up to form a gallery in 1912, but behind, the three grand *salons* of Madame de Pompadour retain their panelling and chimneypieces surmounted by mirrors.

After the Revolution the Prince Joseph de Chimay founded a liberal school, known as *Prytanée* at Ménars, to the east of the *avant-cour*, aimed at bringing together young people of different background and nationalities. Part of this survives together with a small gas manufacturing plant which served to light the college.

Montgeoffroy is a delight. The estate still belongs to the descendants of its builder, the Maréchal de Contades (1704–95), and, remarkably, retains its original furniture and furnishings intact.

The marquis distinguished himself in the sieges of the War of Austrian Succession (1740–48) and received his marshal's baton for leading the infantry to victory at the Battle of Hastembeck at the beginning of the Seven Years War. Quite why he embarked on rebuilding his château at the age of 67, when his duties as Commander in Chief of Alsace kept him away from Anjou, is not clear; the work was probably supervised largely by his son Gaspard (1726–94) and his wife.

Like the Petit Trianon, Montgeoffroy is evidence that the Louis-Seize style had developed, even matured, before the king came to the throne in 1776. Contade's architect was the Parisian, Barré, who worked at Le Lude and the beautiful neo-classical château of Le Marais in the Île de France.

In another sense, however, Montgeoffroy is distinctly *retardataire* or backward-looking, deliberately incorporating elements of the old château to give it a sense of rank and ancestry. A drawing made before the remodelling of

**MONT-
GEOFFROY**

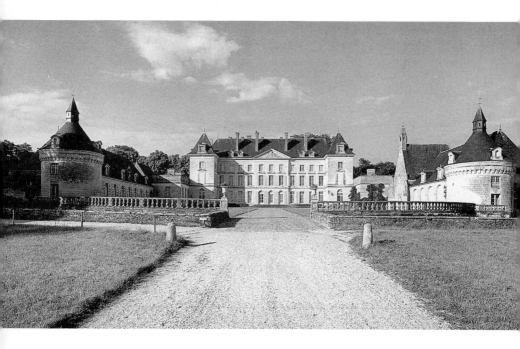

Montgeoffroy: when the château was remodelled in 1772–75, the 16th-century chapel and circular towers were retained.

1772–5 shows a house on an identical plan, with a *cour d'honneur* projecting in a half-moon and approached across a dry moat. Barré retained the circular *poivrières* and the 16th-century Gothic chapel.

The *corps-de-logis* was raised by a storey so the corner towers no longer projected above the main cornice line, and a severe triangular pediment replaced the baroque one. The little wings or pavilions on either side of the towers were given flat roofs and the fenestration regularized. The decorative carving that was the hallmark of Louis-Quinze has disappeared; the emphasis is on contrasting mass and silhouette, balance and harmony.

Inside, carved enrichments are also kept to a minimum. The central **Salon** is a superbly architectural room with the crossed batons of the Maréchal over the doors. The arches of the windows are repeated on the opposite wall, and the mirror over the fireplace matches on the other side of the room. In all, there are no less than five sets of doors, some of which are purely for symmetrical effect. Like all the main apartments the salon is painted in the chaste pearl-grey tones that are the hallmark of Louis-Seize. The inventory drawn up in 1775, as soon as the house was completed (and printed in Pierre Verlet's *La Maison du XVIIIᵉ Siècle en France*) lists no less than 34 chairs and two sofas in the room; these included *fauteuils à la Reine* (with flat backs), four *fauteuils* with square backs, and four *bergères* (filled in beneath the arms) which can still be seen in the room.

The dining-room was something of an innovation in France at that date; the 18th-century practice had been to eat off movable tressels in different rooms. It is dominated by a magnificent faience stove in the shape of a palm tree, with a flat marble top that served as a form of hotplate. Once again the window recesses are repeated in the opposite wall. The double doors at each end, however, are slightly .off-centre, their alignment sacrificed to the greater purpose of the *enfilade* which runs along the garden front.

Opposite the dining-room is the **Appartement de Madame Herrault**—the Maréchal's companion in the

Montgeoffroy: the *salon* retains its Louis-Seize *boiseries* and original furniture.

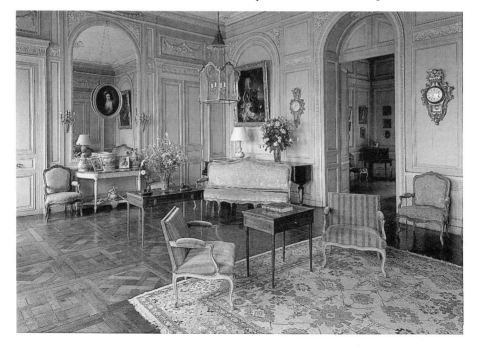

closing years of his life. In this room the austere greys of the Louis-Seize *boiseries* set off admirably the brilliant Venetian brocatelle hangings.

As the Maréchal and Madame Herrault slept on the ground floor, the first floor was reserved entirely for guests. Tall casement windows flood the rooms with light; several of the rooms preserve not only their original furniture, but their hangings intact—beds, curtains, chairs and even walls are all in matching fabrics. The chairs in these rooms are all completely Louis-Seize in character, with oval backs and tapering legs—the characteristic Louis-Quinze cabriolet (S-shaped) legs, to be seen downstairs, are not in evidence. Throughout these guest-rooms strict symmetry reigns, with matching doors set on either side of chimneypieces or bed recesses and the colour of the woodwork everywhere is neo-classical pearl grey.

Outside, as so often in France, the main axis is strongly emphasized; to the south an avenue strides across the landscape as if to pronounce 'this view belongs to me', while on the north side a garden temple is framed by a great avenue of planes.

The visit to Montgeoffroy is completed by the **Harness Room** in one of the *poivrières*, an elegant circular tent fashioned in wood.

MONTPOUPON   Here is an imposing château, set, unusually, on the very edge of the public road, and thereby displayed for all to see at close quarters. The explanation is that it stood guard over the royal route to Spain. A *château fort* occupied the site in 1208, but the present building is no earlier than 1320—the date it came into the hands of the de Prie family, who retained the property till the mid-17th century.

The oldest element is probably the tall circular *donjon* at the west end, complete with machicolations and wall-walk. What is particularly striking is the height of the *corps-de-logis* with four generous storeys of accommodation including the dormers in the roof. This dates back to the 15th century. The whole composition is richly picturesque, with a range of large and small conically-capped

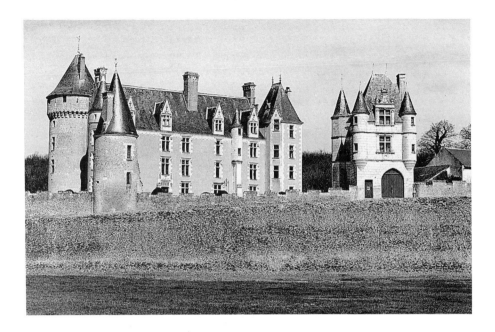

towers, and handsome chimneystacks also complete with machicolations.

The entrance on the road bears the date 1515, marking the return from Italy of Aymard de Prie. The elaborate Renaissance dormer over the entrance, above a Gothic first-floor window, suggests an Italian flourish added by Aymard to the building on his return.

The chapel was demolished in 1793 by the Revolutionaries and substantial restoration was carried out in 1885, for F. L. de La Motte Saint-Pierre, and then in 1920 for his son. To the left of the entrance tower survives one of the original circular towers of the enceinte, set in a battlemented wall.

Montpoupon: the château dates from the early 14th century; the *donjon* is on the left.

On a spur dominating the valley of the Cher, Fulk Nerra, Count of Anjou, built a *donjon* of wood in the 11th century. From Fulk the younger it passed in 1109 to Hugues d'Amboise, who had the *donjon* rebuilt in stone on the model of that at Loches.

The *donjon* is in the typical form of a square tower with

MONT-RICHARD

thick walls reinforced by flat buttresses at the corners and the centre of each floor. This was enclosed by outworks of the same date; a second enceinte was constructed shortly afterwards. In 1188 Philippe Auguste laid siege to the keep and captured it; at this time a third enceinte was added of which only an angle tower remains.

The house of Amboise retained the keep until 1448, and 13 years later it was acquired by Louis XI who built some lodgings near the *donjon*, of which only a round tower survives. The *donjon* was taken by the Catholic League in 1585, but then seized back by the Royalists. On the orders of Henri IV, the upper level, which hid the roof from view, was in part demolished *c.*1600 in order to weaken the defensive capabilities of Montrichard.

Montrichard: the early 12th-century *donjon* stands above the town.

MONTSOREAU

For those who want to sample some of the lesser known and less visited châteaux of the Loire, Montsoreau offers a pleasant interlude, not least because you may explore the place on your own.

If the reconstructions (on show inside) made in 1929 by the curator of the time, the Marquis de Geoffre, are correct, then Montsoreau could have been the most romantic of all the châteaux on the Loire. His drawings, like illustrations from a book of fairytales, show Montsoreau *avec les pieds dans la Loire*—with the river lapping its walls, and diverted round the other three sides to form a moat. Gaignières' view of 1699 shows the walls rising from the Loire, though to the side there is a *parterre* instead of a moat; today, alas, the road has cut off the château from the river, and one is tempted to ask whether this modern convenience need be with us for ever.

In the Middle Ages the owners of Montsoreau held the right to levy dues on river merchandise, and one of them, Jeanne Chabot, brought this right as a dowry on her marriage to Jean de Chambes, Counsellor of Charles VII. The château was reconstructed by them between 1440 and 1445 on a quadrangular plan, but the buildings on three sides have disappeared, with the moats, leaving only the *corps-de-logis* overlooking the Loire.

In 1573 Montsoreau was *érigé en comté'*, raised to the

MONTSOREAU

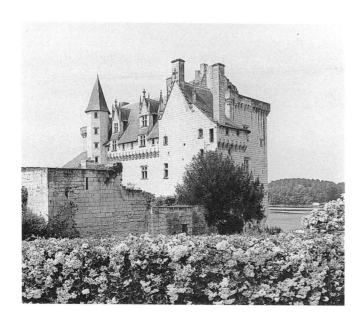

level of an earldom, in favour of Charles de Chambes, the monster who in Anjou directed the 1568 Massacre of Saint Bartholomew in which thousands of Huguenots were murdered. Six years later he trapped his wife's lover, Bussy d'Amboise, Governor of Anjou, in an ambush. This episode, which inspired Dumas' *Dame de Montsoreau*, in fact took place 3 km (2 miles) away at La Coutancière. The château later passed by marriage to the Bouchet de Sourches family. Abandoned after the Revolution, Montsoreau was acquired by the department of Maine-et-Loire in 1913 and from 1918 onwards has been slowly restored by the Monuments Historiques.

The river front still has a feudal aspect with machicolations and intriguing two-tier dormers. In the courtyard, about 1515–20, a beautiful octagonal Renaissance staircase was added, echoing that at Blois, with delicious early Renaissance carving and characteristic panelled pilasters, medallions and sculpted friezes.

Inside, there are some large but otherwise bare rooms. An intriguing period piece is the **Musée des Goums** (Moroccan cavalry regiments) with souvenirs of the pacification of Morocco in 1956.

LA
MORINIÈRE

This is the kind of enchanting small Renaissance manor, on a square island in a square moat, which features so prominently in Holland and Denmark. Here it is all the more appealing because the *corps-de-logis* is on so domestic a scale, and only one room deep.

The château is preceded by a large *avant-cour*, entered through an arch capped by stone balls, and enclosed by farm buildings. Constructed entirely of red brick (with a brick cornice) and red roof tiles it has a wonderful homogenity. The sparing use of stone quoins on corners and around doorways is particularly effective. The best view is to be had by walking around to the left and looking at the house from across the moat. Here there is a delightful well capped with a cupola standing on three Corinthian columns (like a three-legged stool).

The château was probably begun soon after 1528 by René des Roches, seigneur de la Morinière, who inherited from his uncle Ganvin that year, and perhaps completed by 1548, the date on one of the portals. The *corps-de-logis*, though symmetrical in mass, has strangely irregular fenestration and the front door is actually off centre. The

La Morinière: the château was probably completed by 1548, the date on one of the portals.

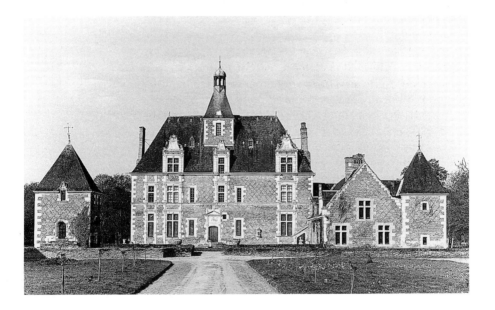

detailing of pilasters and dormers is typical of the early years of the Renaissance. In the 17th century the *cour d'honneur* was entirely closed, but it has subsequently been opened to view. Note the corner pavilions projecting into the moat; that on the left contains the chapel.

As you leave look across to the remarkable brick oven at the centre of a group of farm buildings on your left—which stands like a ruined pyramid by Vanbrugh.

Le Moulin is the perfect moated castle—or would be if its walls were complete. Yet curiously the fact that only fragments survive adds to its picturesque qualities and charm. Seen on a fine day reflected in the still waters of its moat it may leave a deeper impression than many grander châteaux, but in almost any weather it retains the power to captivate.

In 1490 Philippe du Moulin requested a French equivalent of a licence to crenellate. The authorization allowed him to continue the work 'of the last ten or more years'. The master mason in charge of the work in 1501 was Jacques de Persigny from nearby Romorantin. In 1495 Philippe du Moulin had saved the life of Charles VIII at the battle of Fornova in Italy, and the next year Charles gave him the hand in marriage of a rich heiress, Charlotte d'Argouges, widow of Jean d'Harcourt. Subsequently Philippe du Moulin became Chamberlain of France, Counsellor to the King and Governor of Langres, where he died in 1506.

Le Moulin is a brick castle intended to evoke the late-medieval world of chivalry. It has the trappings of feudalism, and a wealth of defensive detail, but can never have been a serious fortification. The smooth round towers flanking the entrance are entirely blind except for a series of narrow gunslits—creating the sense that the building is looking at you as through a vizor. To the left the low connecting wall has the intriguing detail of blank battlements at the level of the windows, while beyond the one surviving corner tower has machicolations and crenellations.

What most appeals is the colour of the building—the

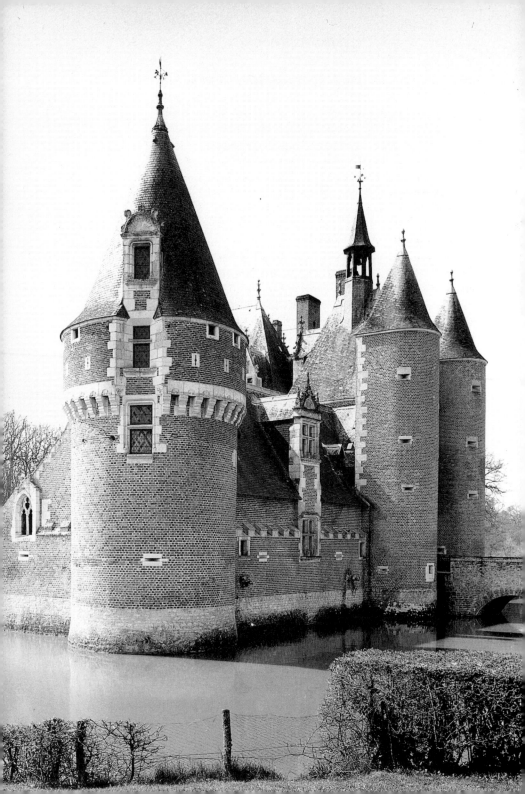

red brick changes colour according to the weather and the time of day—in dull light it has the look of well-worn tweed, on a bright morning it has an orange glow and the diaper patterns in dark brick stand out fiercely.

(Opposite) Le Moulin: the château dates from the last years of the 15th century.

The freestanding *logis* is on an unusual cruciform plan. Internally its character derives from a sensitive restoration carried out in the early years of this century by M. de Marchévile, who bought the property from du Moulin's descendants in 1900. His architects were Charles Genuys, a chief architect for the Monuments Historiques and P. Chauvallon. Genuys introduced an imposing series of Gothic stone chimneypieces—that in the **Salon** is the most elaborate with a rich blind arcade of ogee arches on the hood. These fireplaces were, however, never intended for log fires, each one contains a large ornamental fireback which on closer inspection proves to be a radiator. Here is one of the first, and certainly one of the cleverest, of many forms of disguising central heating and artificial fires. The walls of these rooms are stencilled, and the open beams painted in pleasantly muted colours—a reaction against the much brighter colours of the Gothic revival in the mid-19th century. The elaborate tile floors also date from the restoration.

When you leave, be sure to glance over the white gate set in a clipped hedge at the large well-maintained *potager*.

This is an attractive small château on an L-plan, built in the diapered brick (the darker brick is arranged in a criss-cross pattern) typical of the early 16th century. The arcade on the right with flattened arches bears a distinct resemblance to the Louis XII wing at Blois. However the château was in ruin at the end of the 18th century and was substantially restored by Louis Pepin-Lehalleur who acquired the property in 1848.

NANÇAY

From 1372 to 1766 the estate belonged to the family of La Chêtre. In 1388 it is described as a *maison forte*. In 1413 Jean La Chêtre obtained leave from Duc Jean de Berry to fortify his château, but the work looks almost 100 years later.

Nançay: the château dating from c. 1500 was originally laid out around a courtyard, but only two wings survive.

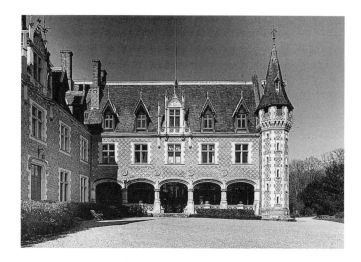

Originally the château was laid out around a courtyard, but the loss of two sides creates a picturesque juxtaposition between the large outside towers and the smaller, conical-hatted inner ones. Note the elaborate dormers and cresting, and the high quality of the stonework.

OIRON

Oiron is a magical place. Its interiors may be empty and unfurnished, all sense of human habitation may have long departed, but magnificent murals, woodwork and plasterwork more than make up for this. An added bonus is that there is no drugget and no ropes, and if you are lucky you will have these great spaces entirely to yourself.

Strictly Oiron is not in the Loire Valley at all, but in Poitou, near Thouars, yet its very splendour means that it is inevitably included in many Loire itineraries.

The château is laid out on three sides of a courtyard with characteristic circular towers punctuating the ends of the wings. The *Seigneurie* was given in 1449, by Charles VII to his chamberlain, Guillaume Gouffier, who founded the family fortunes. He replaced an earlier building with a new château. His second son Guillaume, Admiral of France and favourite of François I, built a magnificent château at Bonnivot in Poitou; his eldest, Artus Gouffier, took part in the Italian expeditions of Charles VIII and

Louis XII and became *gouverneur* (tutor) of the young Comte d'Angoulême, the future François I, who showered him with honours and pensions and named him Grand Master of France.

Before his sudden death in 1519 Artus had built the open gallery on the left (as you approach) of the *cour d'honneur*. This is still Gothic in style, inspired by the Blois of Louis XII, with shallow arches and spirally fluted columns. Within, there is an elaborately vaulted roof with ribs springing not from bosses, but directly from the walls, in the final abstract mode of Gothic (note the way the ribs interlace as they 'die' into the walls).

The widow of Artus, Hélène de Hangest, continued the construction of the collegiate chapel he had just begun. This was completed in 1542. Flamboyant Gothic in style, with delicate Renaissance detail, it houses a splendid series of family tombs. Their son, Claude Gouffier, enjoyed royal favour: he became *Premier Gentilhomme de la Chambre* in 1535, *Capitaine des Cent Gentilhommes* in 1545, and *Grand Écuyer* the next year. In 1566 he was created Duc de Roannais.

Oiron was his favourite residence and his first work was to add a magnificent first-floor gallery over the Gothic

Oiron: the cour d'honneur of the 16th-century château.

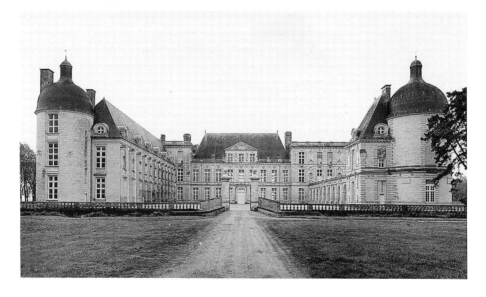

arcade. His Renaissance detail is ingeniously added to make it look, at first glance, a single design. The large mullioned windows (with octagonal lead panes) have classical surrounds; the niches in between formerly housed terracotta terms (one survives in the Louvre, others in America). Below the windows are portrait medallions of the Caesars and more unexpectedly of Mahomet.

The paintings on the walls inside the gallery date from 1545–49, and were painstakingly conserved between 1956–71. With Fontainebleau and Ancy-le-France they are the most remarkable 16th-century murals in France. The artist is known only by name: Noël Jallier. They portray scenes from the *Aeneid* and the *Iliad*; note the *trompe-l'oeil* touch of the drapes hanging over the frames.

Claude Gouffier also added the staircase at the left end of the *corps-de-logis* in 1542–44 and rebuilt the circular tower at the other end with a dome in 1548–50. Originally there was a second floor over the gallery, with large dormers, but this was replaced in the 17th century by *oeils-de-boeuf* windows.

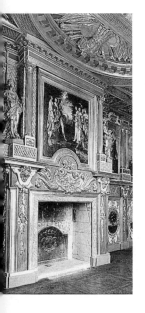

One of the splendid chimneypieces at Oiron.

Claude died in 1570, shortly after the château had been sacked by the Protestants. His grandson, Louis Gouffier, Duc de Roannais, carried out further major work and reconstructed the *corps-de-logis*. His grandson, Artus III, mathematician and friend of Pascal, retired to a monastery and left Oiron to his sister, who in 1667, married François d'Aubusson, who, to flatter Louis XIV, erected the monument in the Place des Victoires, Paris. At Oiron between 1670–80 he completed the *corps-de-logis*, and encased the early 16th-century stair in a new pavilion.

The rich interiors of the **Chambre du Roi** and the **Cabinet des Muses** are of this date. François d'Aubusson also built the low wing on the right. He died in 1691, and his son sold Oiron in 1700 to the Marquise de Montespan. In 1739 the château was sold to the Marquis de Villeroy, then from 1772 right up to 1941 it was in the hands of the Fournier de Boisairault family. Oiron's spell lies largely in the fact that from the 18th century the château in effect went to sleep, to be preserved in this condition until 1941 when it was acquired by the state.

Le Plessis-Bourré is a charming example of a 15th-century manor house parading as a castle. The harmony of its architecture stems largely from the fact that it was built in just five years, between 1468 and 1473. Jean Bourré (1424–1506) had acquired the *domaine* in 1462. He was a counsellor and treasurer of Louis XI, and later *Secrétaire des Finances* to Charles VIII and Louis XII.

The approach is given added appeal by the *communs*, rebuilt in the 17th century in three ranges to form an *avant-cour*. By contrast to the courtly grandeur of much Loire architecture this is engagingly provincial, suggesting the hand of a local mason who did not exactly work out his measurements and his axis.

The château stands in a broad, square moat and is approached across a long, shallow-arched bridge. In the gatehouse the levers and chains to raise the carriage and footbridges survive and fold back neatly into recesses in the walls. As so often, one of the towers is taller than the

LE PLESSIS-BOURRÉ

Le Plessis-Bourré: the moated château dates principally from 1468–73.

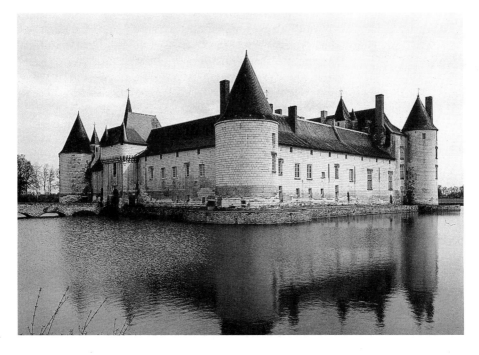

others, playing the part of the *donjon*. Here it has the additional set-back storey also found at Langeais (of which Jean Bourré was *capitaine*).

The *corps-de-logis* at the back of the courtyard is not symmetrical, but has the tall dormers characteristic of Flamboyant Gothic. The chapel, marked by its tall roof, stands to the left of the entrance arch. Inside the house, the **Salle des Gardes** has a remarkable late Gothic coffered ceiling painted with scenes of proverbs.

In 1911 Le Plessis-Bourré was acquired by M. Henri Vaisse, who carefully repaired the building and introduced a series of handsome Louis-Quinze and Louis-Seize *boiseries* in various rooms.

PONT-
CHEVRON

Pont-Chevron is a perfect period piece, though of a rather different date than most châteaux of the Loire—1896–1900 to be exact. Designed by the architects Coulomb and Chauvet for Louis d'Harcourt, the formal landscaping and planting that formed an integral part of the whole design has now matured and is at its best.

You catch an inviting diagonal glimpse of the entrance front from the lodge. Here is a ravishing marriage of architecture, sculpture and gardens; the *parterres*, surrounded by gravel paths, exactly match the width of the main front and are framed by neatly clipped hedges punctuated by urns backed by lines of carefully pleached beech, swinging out in a half circle beside the main front.

The access for visitors, however, is through the *communs* facing the house. One side was for the horses, the other for the cars. Two pavilions stand at the ends; one contains a chapel—note how the creeper has been clipped to fit the arches.

Beyond the house, the lawns slope down to a magnificent naturalistically contoured lake, as large as any by Capability Brown. The *parterres* on the lake side, studded with neat pincushions of box, once again match the width of the house, and are flanked by tunnels of lime. The whole composition in its precise linearity corresponds with the contemporary pavilion built by Alfred Dupont I at Nemours, near Wilmington in Delaware, USA.

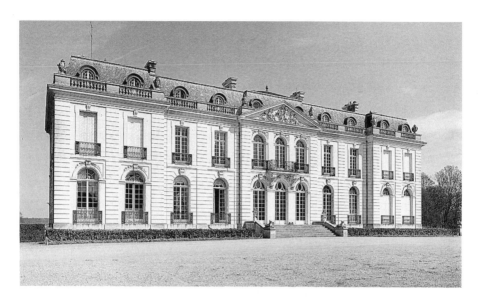

And this is the point about the architecture of the house—it could equally stand in America or Europe: here is the polished Louis-Quinze/Louis-Seize revival of the Ritz and the grand spa towns of central Europe. It has echoes too of 18th-century châteaux like Jossigny, Omonville, Champs-sur-Marne and Champletreaux. The entrance steps are flanked by superbly sculpted hounds, the pediment contains a lively high relief of a bacchanal of *putti*. The garden front is treated in a similar manner with a rotunda capped by a shallow dome. The size of the dormers is cleverly concealed by cladding them in lead which merges with the roof.

The entrance hall is very much a continuation of the exterior with white channelled stonework and an equally brilliant floor, opening directly into a sweeping staircase with the richly swagged columns that are a signature of the age. The oval dining-room lined with fluted *scagliola* pilasters looks over the lake and in a nearby room there is, naturally, a large billiard-table.

While some houses of 1900 date are just a little overblown with the pretensions of Empire, Pont-Chevron, has the elegance and aptness of scale of a house where comfort was as important as style.

119

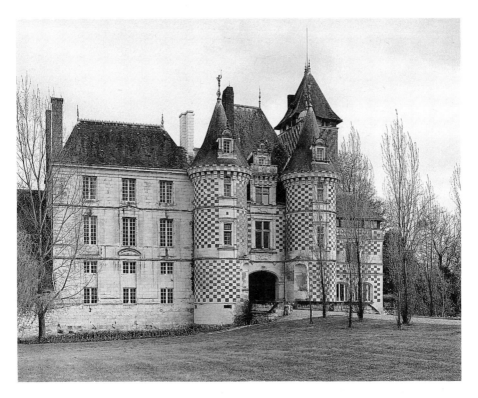

LES RÉAUX

This is a small château of exceptional charm thanks largely to its engaging chequer livery and cluster of steep roofs.

It is sometimes said to be the work of Guillaume Briçonnet, superintendent of Finances for Charles VIII, who acquired the estate at the end of the 15th century, possibly when he received his cardinal's hat in 1495. However the style is unquestionably that of the reign of François I—note for example the pilasters on the windows of the towers and the shell-headed dormers. These features suggest a date after Guillaume's death in 1514 and the house is likely to be the work of his son, Jean, who died in 1559.

The chequerboard effect, though distinctive, is not exceptional at this date; more unusual are the diagonal 'arrowhead' stripes on the top of the *donjon* behind.

The wing on the left of the entrance was built for Louis Taboureau, a royal counsellor, who bought the property in 1714 (his family arms were added to the entrance of the *donjon*). The lower wing on the right of the main entrance was added (and designed) by Julien Barois who bought the château in 1897, in the same style as the original 16th-century work. The chapel in the courtyard is in a neo-Renaissance style.

RIVAULDE

This is another of the mighty early 20th-century châteaux of the Sologne. Constructed in red brick with a flecking of white stone trim, it looks more like a military academy than a *rendez-vous de chasse*. It was built in 1902 for Mme Schneider to the designs of the architect Coulon. It is on a V-plan, or if you count the bays of the bows on the garden front, an X-plan; this suggests an intriguing parallel, which must at this date be deliberate, to one of the greatest of all hunting lodges, Stupinigi outside Turin, built between 1729–35. Stupinigi has the diagonal advancing wings and central domed tower, with arched windows in the upper storey.

However, Coulon is playing a subtle game, for his balancing wings and corner pavilions are each treated quite differently—for example, on the left the pediments of the upper windows just break through the cornice, on the right there are full dormers.

The Château de Rivaulde built in 1902.

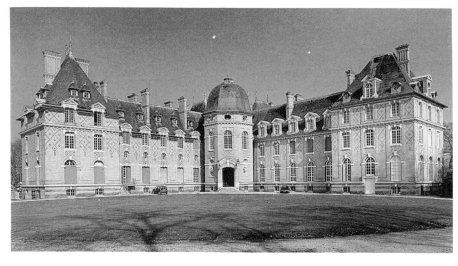

Part of the appeal of Rivaulde is the very high quality of the materials and craftsmanship at this date, and the attractive colour of the brick. This continues inside in the combined staircase and entrance hall; the oval stair winds back over the entrance (in a manner similar to the delightful 18th-century Château de Bagatelle at Abbeville).

The château de Rivaulde is being given a new life as the club house of a very smart golf course and vast landscaping works have been carried out in the park. Not an inch of space is wasted: the circle of grass in front of the entrance has become a putting green.

The château is marked by a white rectangle on the D 724 just outside Salbris, which is some 50 km (30 miles) south of Orléans on the N 20.

SAUMUR

Whichever way your approach, Saumur is a wonderful sight. From across the Loire, it towers over river and town; seen from the south the château dominates the entire flat landscape, its elevation, size and symmetry imbuing it with regal grandeur.

The excitement of seeing it is heightened by the fact that this is one of the few châteaux in *Les Très Riches Heures du Duc de Berry* (c.1410, the most beautiful of all medieval illuminated manuscripts) which can both be identified and recognized today. But before your hopes are raised too high be warned that in the 18th century the château was a prison and in the 19th a barracks, with all the depredations that these uses inevitably involved.

A château was first built here in the 12th century by Geoffroy Plantaganet. In 1207 it became royal property under King Philippe Auguste; in 1246 St Louis gave it to his brother Charles. At this time the château assumed a quadrangular plan with circular towers.

In 1360 Jean le Bon elevated Anjou to a hereditary duchy in favour of his son Louis, who preferred Saumur to Angers. He set about creating a princely residence rivalling the luxuriousness of those of his brother King Charles V and that of Jean, Duc de Berry, at Mehun-sur-Yevre (also illustrated in *Les Très Riches Heures*).

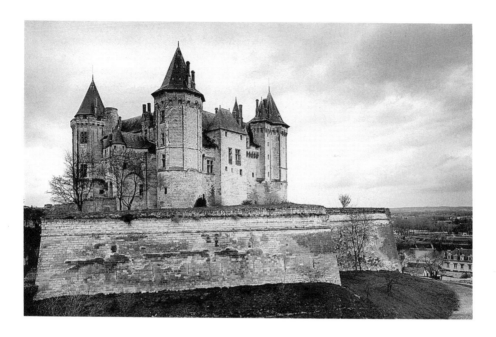

The 13th-century angle towers became polygonal, emphasized at the corners by shallow pilasters which survive today. The manuscript view shows the kind of romantic silhouette that Disney has taken over and made his trademark: battlemented towers capped by conical roofs, carrying fleurs-de-lis finials, a forest of precarious chimneys and ornate dormers (see p.7).

Looking at the house from the modern car park you can recognize the main elements in the manuscript view: the projecting entrance guarded by a barbican, the polygonal towers and a lower square tower on the east side.

King René (d.1480), grandson of Louis I d'Anjou, rebuilt part of the château between 1454–72, adding an octagonal staircase at the eastern angle of the *corps-de-logis*. On his death the property reverted to the crown. Henri IV appointed the Protestant leader Philippe de Mornay governor of Saumur and he lived here in princely fashion, furnishing the château with tapestries and a famous collection of portraits. His departure in 1621, was followed by abandonment, and the west range collapsed, never to be rebuilt.

Saumur: the château assumed its present form in the late 14th century.

After the spell as prison and barracks, the château was bought by the town of Saumur and restored as a museum. For your ticket you will gain admission to the rather plain courtyard and have a guided tour of the **Museum of Decorative Arts** and the **Equine Museum** devoted to the history of the horse and horsemanship.

SERRANT

You will need to be hawk-eyed to catch the grand *coup d'œil* of Serrant on the Angers-Nantes road, an axial vista through a screen of railings framed by four lines of chestnuts on either side. The château stands on a large square platform set in a broad, deep-set moat, crossed by bridges on three sides. Beyond, the grounds open into a large verdant park.

For all the formality of the layout, and regularity of its architecture, Serrant evolved over several centuries. A château was built here in 1481 by Ponthus de Brie, chamberlain of Louis XI, on the site of a medieval predecessor. A view of 1695 by Gaignières shows two circular towers guarding the entrance. His grandson, Charles de Brie, began an ambitious remodelling attributed (though there is no documentary evidence) to Philibert de l'Orme. By his death in 1593 only the left-hand part of the *corps-de-logis* and the centre with the main staircase had been completed.

In 1636 Serrant was acquired by Guillaume de Bautru (1588–1665) who completed the *corps-de-logis* and added the two projecting wings. The two freestanding pavilions at the corners came later, one before the 1695 watercolour, one after. The handsome central entrance arch carries the arms—a swan—of François Jacques Walsh, who was created Count of Serrant by Louis XV in 1755.

Serrant had been bought for him by his brother Antoine, Earl Walsh, an Irish arms manufacturer, who was created an Irish peer by James III. Reversing the steps of the Huguenots the Walshes had established themselves in Nantes in 1688 when James II had fled, and remained loyal to the Stuarts. Another Antoine, son of François, supplied two ships for Bonnie Prince Charlie's 1745 Rebellion.

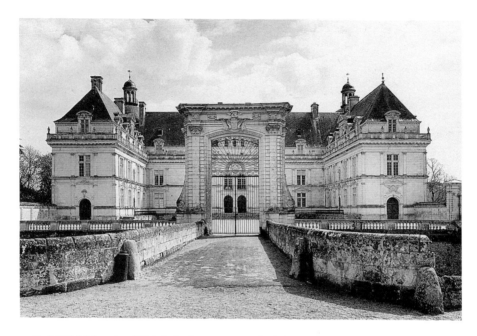

In 1830 Valentine Walsh de Serrant married the Duc de
La Trémoïlle, and it was the Duke who commissioned an
extensive programme of restoration by the architect
Lucien Magre. He took off the top storey of the
corps-de-logis and wings and replaced them with a series
of powerful lucarnes set behind a balustrade topped with
urns.

For all these many alterations Serrant is a grand unified
composition and there is a striking contrast between the
dark brown rough schist used for the exterior and the
white stone of the courtyard.

The *corps-de-logis* has the usual early Renaissance
arrangement of an order of pilasters to each storey, Ionic
then Corinthian. The exuberance of the early Renaissance
has been succeeded by a concern for correctness, and
there is even perhaps a touch of *'froideur'*. There are
nonetheless nice architectural details—such as the fan
motifs in the pediments above the little windows of the
towers, and the full Doric entablature on the screen wall
by the side entrance. Serrant's two massive cylindrical
towers, recall Valençay, and carry powerful bell domes

Serrant: the *cour
d'honneur* seen from
across the moat.

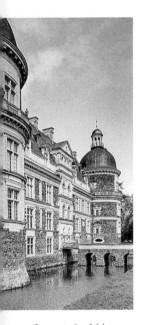

Serrant: the 16th-century front overlooking the park.

and open cupolas. Note the large oval gunports in the foot of the towers.

The front doors open into a splendid barrel-vaulted stone staircase and it is the sophistication of the architectural treatment here which suggests de l'Orme (best known for his work at Anet for Diane de Poitiers). De l'Orme was a master of perspective effects on ceilings and domes, and deep cross-pattern coffering (diamond over the landing) speaks of an architect who could draw out highly sophisticated patterns. Similar vaults are found in the tower rooms. Also typical of him is the continuous stylobate carrying the pilasters on the stair.

For all its grandeur, the *corps-de-logis* proves to be only one room deep; in the left-hand room, is the **Antichambre**; note the way the double doors are 'faked' to match the stair. Beyond, the **Bedroom of the Prince de Tarante** is interesting for the way a bathroom has been contrived within a cupboard, while the lavatory is concealed in a closet in the window reveal.

The rooms on the upper floor impress with their enormous height and huge chimneypieces. The library, furnished as a family room, has up to 16 tiers of books, with a continuous rail for a ladder. The bolection mouldings suggest a date towards 1700. Across the staircase the **Grand Salon** has an intriguing star-pattern ceiling of 1900 in Italian chestnut, suggesting a visit to the Alhambra at Granada. Note the bookcases at the end, built to hold leather archive boxes. The *parquet à la française* has elaborate brass grilles—evidence of an underfloor heating system, introduced around 1850 and apparently still in use.

Beyond lies the **Bedroom** furnished for Napoleon's visit in 1808, with handsome Empire furniture, all upholstered *en suite*, and elaborate wallpaper borders.

Students of the mechanics of country-house life should look out for the remarkable hand-operated lift of 1900 at the end of the wing, built into a handsome wooden staircase well of the same date.

At the end of the wing on the opposite side of the courtyard is the chapel, sometimes attributed to Hardouin Mansart, architect of Versailles. With its black marble pilasters set against white stonework it makes a splendid setting for the monument by Antoine Coysevox to the Marquis de Vaubran, son-in-law, of the second de Bautru, killed in 1675 at the battle of Altenheim. The hero lies wounded in the field while Victory descends from the skies to place a laurel wreath on his brow. The black marble panels in the pedestals beneath the pilasters record a sadder event: the death of five children from tuberculosis. The family pew on a balcony to the left, with an upholstered rail, is entered directly from the château.

On leaving the château, walk round to admire the large lake in the English style, approached by balustraded steps on the axis of the garden front. At the end of the stable block is a large circular dovecote overlooking a large rectangular pool. This has a noble stone dome and open cupola with grass sprouting romantically from the roof. Byzantium has arrived on the Loire.

Arriving at Sully you have the impression it stands in a moat, unusually large perhaps; but if you set out to walk round surprise awaits, for the southern arm continues out of sight to the east as a gentle river. Sully, in fact, stands at the confluence of the River Sange with the Loire, with its great park stretched out along the peninsula between. The first island is now bare of buildings, but was once the site of a *donjon* built by Philippe Auguste shortly before 1219, as well as the collegiate church of Saint-Ythier which the Duc de Sully moved to the town.

The present château is a composition of extraordinary power, for once a real fortress rather than a glorious chivalrous display. The property came by marriage in 1382 to the Poitevin family of La Trémoïlle, who built the present *donjon* known as the **Vieux Château**, looking north towards the Loire, and punctuated at the corners by four massive cylindrical towers. Guy de La Trémoïlle's architect was the celebrated Raymond du Temple, architect of the King and the Duc d'Orléans, who transformed the Louvre for Charles V. The entrance, flanked by small towers, is on the south side in the courtyard.

SULLY-SUR-LOIRE

Sully: the massive steep-roofed *donjon*, dating from c. 1400, is on the left.

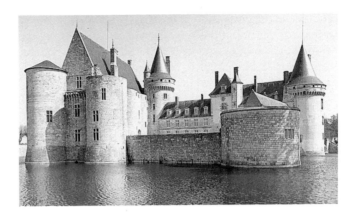

The wing with the present entrance tower, approached across the moat, is known as the **Petit Château**, and dates from the 16th century. Confusingly the short range between the entrance tower and the Vieux Château was built in the 18th century, and then given machicolations and a wall-walk after a fire in 1918.

Sully is, above all, associated with Henri IV's great minister Maximilien de Béthune, Marquis de Rosny, for whom Sully was raised in 1606 to a duchy—the Duc de Sully was charged with the reconstruction of the kingdom after the devastation of the Wars of Religion. He was Superintendent of Finances and Buildings and Grand Master of Artillery and his work at Sully parallels that of Charles II de Condé, Governor of Paris, whom Henri IV created Duc de Brissac, at his great château near Angers. 'If you do not return to Paris in two years time', wrote Malherbe of Béthune's work in 1605 'you will no longer be able to recognize it'.

Sully built the low, flat-topped artillery tower, the **Tour de Béthune**, overlooking the town at the south-west, as well as remodelling the interior of the *donjon*. In the **Grand Salon** is a vast bird's-eye view of the family château of Rosny at Yvelines on the Seine, west of Paris, showing the house and formal garden, painted directly on the hood of the fireplace. Next door, the 17th-century decoration of the **King's Room** with *faux* panelling and a state bed with brilliant blue hanging, has recently been recreated. The iron door on the south side originally opened into Sully's

128

cabinet, though today it is presented as a chapel with replicas of the statues of Sully and his second wife in the Hotel Dieu at Nogent-le-Rotron.

On the upper level the magnificent roof space is so large that it is a hall in itself, with the timbers rising vertically from the floor and arching over like an upturned hull in an almost continuous curve. Though strictly utilitarian it is as spectacular a forest of medieval roof timbers as is to be found in France. From here you emerge onto the wall-walk over the Loire and look down between the planks directly into the waters of the moat.

In the range to the south of the entrance the lodgings of the Duc de Sully are shown, but in fact the rooms are, as is evident from the woodwork and painted decoration, entirely a recreation of the 19th century. Note the chimneypiece with the Master of Artillery's flaming cannon balls, and the eagle with the lightning of Jupiter and the motto, paying homage to Henri IV 'I go wherever Jupiter orders'. After Henri IV's assassination Sully lived principally on his estates, dictating his famous *Mémoires* which were printed here in 1641, the year of his death.

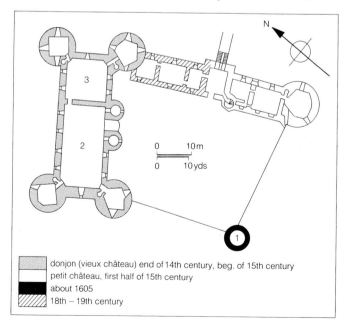

donjon (vieux château) end of 14th century, beg. of 15th century
petit château, first half of 15th century
about 1605
18th – 19th century

Sully-sur-Loire
1. Tour de Béthune
2. Grand salon
3. King's room

In the 18th century Voltaire spent three years at Sully, where his tragedy *Arthemisa* was staged for the first time in the Grand Salon. Damaged by fire in 1918 and bombarded in the Second World War the château has been carefully repaired and was acquired in 1962 by the Département du Loiret, which has continued the work of restoration.

TALCY

The château stands in a little village street, only barely set back from the pavement and bordered by a line of pleached trees. It is laid out around a courtyard and built against the village church.

In 1517 the property was acquired by a Florentine banker, Bernard Salviati, with close connections to the King. Three years later, on 12 September 1520, Salviati obtained the French equivalent of an English licence to

Talcy: the courtyard of the early 16th-century château.

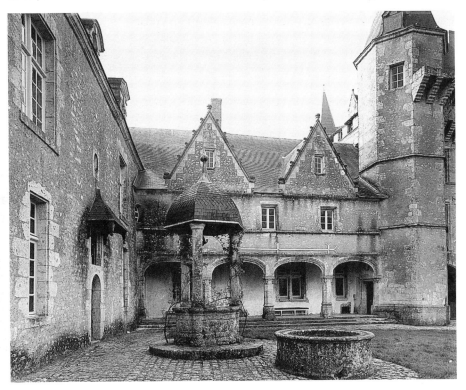

crenellate—the right to construct a *maison forte* with towers, barbicans, machicolations, gunloops, drawbridges and other defensive elements. However only the square gatehouse with its embattled wall-walk fits the descriptions; and more surprising still there is none of the Renaissance detail (as at Azay and Chenonceau) which one might have expected to be added by a rich financier moving in court circles, and an Italian at that. It may therefore be that the larger part of the work was completed by earlier owners, either Jean Simon, bishop of Paris, who died in 1502, or his wife who continued to live here until 1517.

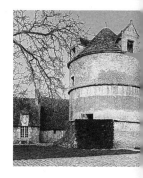

Talcy: the dovecote.

Internally the entrance range has an arcade characteristic of the early 16th century with flattened arches resting on octagonal columns, while the gables above bear the remains of Gothic crockets. Inside the house the rooms have open-beam ceilings and are attractively arranged with 16th- and 18th-century furniture. In the courtyard is a pretty well with a cupola resting on three columns, similar to that at La Morinière. There is also a well-preserved 16th-century dovecote similar to that at Serrant.

Ussé is one of those houses which bears the stamp of many successive owners. Over the centuries these have changed a powerful brooding fortress into a luxurious country house, overlooking a magnificent formal garden laid out in terraces dropping down to the river.

The silhouette is intensely romantic seen from across the Loire, with as many clustered towers and pointed roofs as in an illustration from *Les Très Riches Heures du Duc de Berry*. It is said that the famous writer of fairy stories, Charles Perrault, based the setting for *Sleeping Beauty* on Ussé. But for all the profusion of stylistic elements the architectural evolution is relatively straightforward.

The large cylindrical tower at the south-west corner is built on the foundations of an earlier medieval building. To this was added a château on a quadrangular plan, punctuated at the corners by circular towers. Ussé, like Langeais and Chaumont, has a corner entrance flanked by

USSÉ

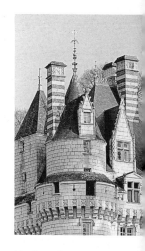

Ussé: roofscape.

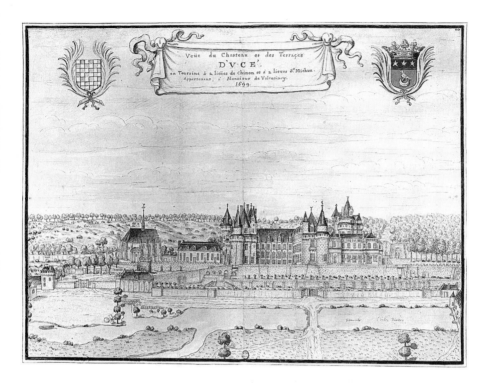

Veüe du Chasteau et des Terrasses
D'VCE'.
en Touraine à 2 lieües de Chinon et à 2 lieües St. Michau.
Appartenant à Monsieur de Valrutincy.
1699.

Ussé: the château and formal gardens recorded in 1699 by Gaignières.

twin cylindrical towers—though here it has been blocked. As at Langeais the upper stage of the towers is set back. Later, again like Chaumont, the wing overlooking the Indre and the Loire was demolished to open up a view of the river.

The builders were Jean V de Bueil (died 1477) and his son, Antoine, who sold Ussé in 1485 to Jacques d'Espinay, chamberlain of Louis XII. His son, Charles d'Espinay, succeeded in 1523 and completed the west wing of the courtyard in Renaissance style.

Charles d'Espinay also built the beautiful collegiate chapel following his father's last wishes. This is still Flamboyant Gothic, but with a very rich Renaissance portal surmounted by a giant *coquille*. The chapel bears the initials C and L for Charles d'Espinay and his wife Lucrèce de Pons, who died in 1535; the building was consecrated three years later. The rich contemporary stalls were restored *c.*1885.

Ussé passed in 1659 to the family of Bertine de Valentinay, who opened up the courtyard, built the terraces and the orangery. These alterations are shown in a view by Gaignières, dated 1699. Louis II, Bernin de Valentinay, married the sister of Vauban, the famous military engineer, and these works are sometimes attributed to him—though no documentary evidence exists.

A thoroughgoing restoration was undertaken in the 19th century by the Comtesse de la Rochejacquelain, who owned the property from 1829–1883. The east front, for all its array of machicolations, battlements and gunloops, has a rather hard quality.

Inside, the main staircase is 17th-century, as is the **Chambre du Roi**, which was designed originally for Louis XIV. This room has a screen of gilded Corinthian columns and a handsome *lit à la polonaise* with a domed canopy.

Valençay is properly in Berry, but has for so long been a major sight for visitors to the Loire that it must be included here.

VALENÇAY

The approach is grand enough for a Royal Palace and reminds me of the Summer Palace of the Danish kings at Rosenborg, outside Stockholm. The main street of the town is aligned on the château and planted with an *allée* of giant plane trees which arch over like the nave of a cathedral. At the end, a screen of railings with gilt arrowheads announces the *domaine* and the street sweeps off deferentially to the left. Inside, a second *allée* of chestnuts frames the view, opening into a large oval service court. The mass of trees here forms an extension of the architecture almost obscuring the triangular courts of stable and farm buildings. Worth a glance is the semi-circular stable through the further arch on the left.

Intriguingly, the bones of this layout are already shown in Gaignières' view of 1705; Valençay's stupendous layout was envisaged from the start. The early history of the château lies with the Estampes family, five generations of whom held lucrative government office and married heiresses.

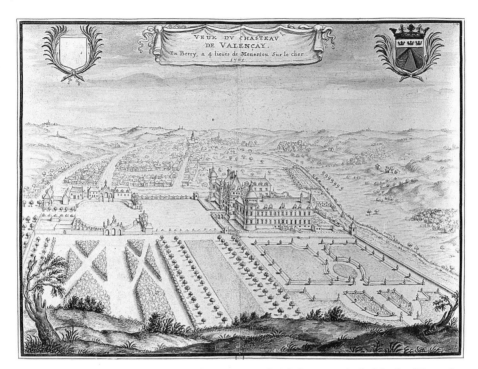

VEUE DV CHASTEAV DE VALENÇAY.
En Berry, a 4 lieües de Menestou Sur le cher 1705.

Gaignières' view of Valençay, 1705.

Valençay: the earliest part of the château is this tower.

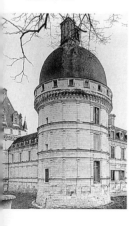

Louis, Governor of Blois, married Marie Hurault, daughter of the Seigneur of Cheverny in 1512; Jacques, born in 1518, married in 1540 the daughter of a financier; Jean, born in 1548, married the sole heiress of a great Picardy family, Sara d'Happlaincourt, and became Governor of Montpellier. His son, Dominique, 1st Marquis de Valençay et d'Happlaincourt, married the daughter of François de Montmorency-Bouteville. After this decline set in, and in 1747 Valençay was sold, passing in 1766 to a *fermier-général*, Legendre de Villemorien, whose son in 1803 sold the estate to Napoleon's great foreign minister Talleyrand. It is said that Napoleon shared the cost of the château as it was intended that Talleyrand should entertain foreign ambassadors and other important guests here.

The north-facing entrance front (strictly NNW) clearly speaks of interrupted works and changes of mind. The earliest part of the château is the large cylindrical tower on the right, which, with its three tiers of flat, widely spaced pilasters, is very similar to Chambord. Recently, two

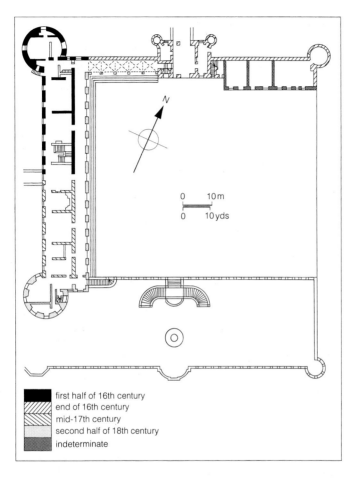

Valençay

first half of 16th century
end of 16th century
mid-17th century
second half of 18th century
indeterminate

small rooms on the ground and first floors have been found to have ceilings with the arms of Louis d'Estampes (who died in 1530) and Marie Hurault, suggesting Valençay was begun in the 1520s. At the same time, roughly half the existing north and west ranges were constructed—the delicious early Renaissance detail is visible inside the courtyard. It is suggested that the large tower's machicolations (not found at Chambord) and powerful bell-dome followed the marriage of Jacques d'Estampes in 1540. The dome thus corresponds in date as well as shape with that at Gué-Péan, begun soon after 1543. From this develops the hypothesis that the château was originally intended to be smaller, with shorter ranges between four circular towers—echoing Chambord, perhaps with the entrance on the east, facing the centre of the town.

Valençay's present entrance tower, in the form of a large *donjon*, carries the date 1599 on one of the dormers as well as the arms of d'Happlaincourt. Yet the Renaissance detail is puzzlingly that of the first half of the century. Is the entrance tower, therefore, an example of intentionally backward-looking architecture, intended to proclaim ancestry and romance? The new grand plan as shown in Gaignières' view was evidently never completed, though an east wing was built but is thought to have been demolished in the 18th century. Gaignières' drawing is also evidence that the south-west cylindrical tower came later, though at this date the west wing had already been extended to its present length.

The building of the south-west tower—and the courtyard front of the west range—can be ascribed to the *fermier-général*. His architect was Joseph-Abel Couture, who in the letter accompanying his candidature for the Academy in 1767, cites 'the grand extensions, embellishments, decoration, park, garden, kitchen garden, canals, terrace and plantation at the Château de Valençay'.

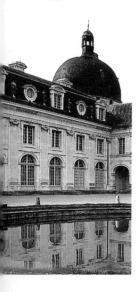

Valençay: this range in the inner courtyard was re-fronted in the 1760s.

The new front in the courtyard, with its elegant fluted pilasters, is fully neo-classical (what is called Louis-Seize, though Louis XVI only succeeded in 1774), without a trace of the rococo of Louis-Quinze. Simplicity and calm now reign: the façade is flat for its full length (apart from the slightest of breaks in the centre) and the cornice line unwavering. Huge classical urns stand on the parapet, alternating with boldly architectural dormers. The carved detail is now restricted entirely to the orders—note the swags to the capitals and the *coquilles* at the top of the cornice.

In this, Couture is perhaps inadvertently echoing the game played by his Renaissance predecessor on the adjoining wing—where the frieze is stretched to include a blind balustrade. Within the arcade the vaulting is essentially Gothic. Note the elaborate Mannerist door at one end.

Inside, the work of the Renaissance and 18th century (at least in the rooms on show) has largely disappeared, and the elaborate *boiseries* date mainly from Talleyrand's period, or even later, as is evinced by the plate glass in the windows, and nice chased steel window-handles.

Here Talleyrand assembled a fine collection of Empire furniture, while Ferdinand VII, dethroned King of Spain, was detained here by Napoleon between 1808–14. The **Grand Salon**, with its screen of columns, looks as if it was created by two rooms being thrown together in the 19th century. The **Duchess Room** in the tower shows the French passion for symmetry carried to its extreme with so many matching pairs of double doors and mirrors that there is no wall space left for furniture or pictures. Upstairs, the main point of interest is the horseshoe-shaped **King's Bedroom**, hung with a superb series of *grisaille*-painted wallpapers of *The Life of Psyche*, made by J. Dufour in Paris between 1814–1815. These were designed by L. Lafitte and M.J. Blondel, and have superb architectural backdrops (in all, 12 scenes are recorded).

From the upstairs windows you have a fine view over the deerpark and the lower park and have a glimpse of the half-moon **Rendezvous de Chasse** by Jacques-Charles Bonnard.

VILLANDRY

For anyone interested in the design of formal gardens—past or present—Villandry can only be described as *éclatant*—positively dazzling. Yet it is not to everyone's taste: one of my companions once expressed horror at 'this prison camp for flowers'.

The gardens of Villandry as they appear today are not a restoration, but a completely new creation, undertaken by a Spaniard, Dr Joachim Carvallo and his American wife Anne Coleman. They bought the estate in 1906, and saved the château from probable demolition and division into building lots.

The *donjon* of the medieval Château de Coulombiers survives at the south-west corner of the present building. This was retained by Jean Breton (or Le Breton) who began reconstructing the château in 1532 in typical

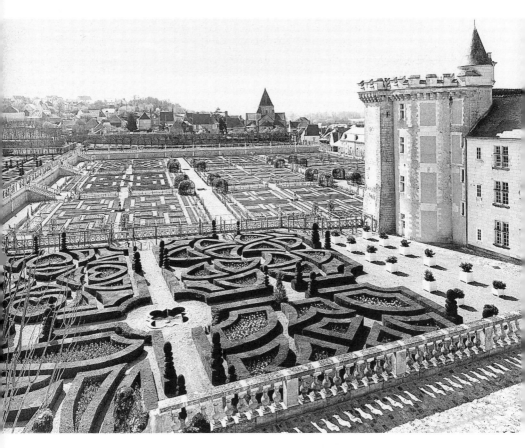

A view over Villandry's formal gardens which were laid out early this century.

Renaissance style with steep roofs, tall dormers and windows flanked by pilasters. Le Breton was, like so many of the Renaissance builders, a financier, President of the Chambres des Comptes at Blois, and also builder of the Château de Villesavin.

In 1754 the new owner, the Marquis Michel-Ange de Castellane, embarked on an extensive remodelling, shown in photographs taken about 1900. He opened up the quadrangle towards the Loire (as at Ussé and Chaumont) and completely changed the character of the château by introducing casement windows in every available blank space of wall. The 1900 photographs also show a roof pavilion and balustrade on top of the *donjon*.

Carvallo, by turn, eliminated virtually every trace of the

18th-century work, reinstating the panels of plain stone between the original windows to recreate the Renaissance character. He reopened the moats, removing the terrace Castellane had introduced.

Carvallo's major work—in scale and accomplishment not to be superseded until the reinstatement of the baroque gardens at Het Loo in Holland in the 1980s—was in the gardens. Here is the one 16th-century château with gardens of the size, complexity and elaboration shown in engravings by du Cerceau. But though Villandry was known to have had elaborate gardens in the 16th century, no visual record survived and Carvallo modelled his new garden particularly on du Cerceau's views of Bury and Fontainebleau.

The two main axes of the garden are those laid down by Castellane about 1762, (recorded in a plan in the departmental archives), but also evident on the ground not least from stonework details. Carvallo retained the large 18th-century basin at the top of the garden (simplifying its shape) and the canal leading to the moat. Though the design appears absolutely regular and geometric, most of the *parterres* are trapezoidal in form, but this is concealed by perspective.

Carvallo, born in 1869, had studied medicine in Madrid and Paris, where he met his future wife, also a medical student. They married in 1899 and the death of her parents provided the funds for them to retire to the country.

Curiously the liberal ideas of Carvallo's youth were succeeded when it came to gardening by a rather authoritarian and unattractively expressed concept of hierarchy. He explained this in a preface to Prosper Péan's *Jardins de France* in 1924.

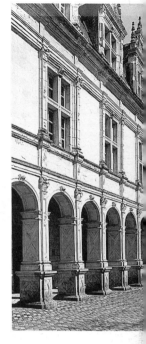

Part of the courtyard of the 16th-century château, which was restored to its original appearance early this century.

> Our ancestors had a different conception of life from ours . . . the various elements of domestic order each had its place . . . animals were lower than the servants, and the servants were not on a level with the workers . . . The 19th century imbued with the principles of an absurd egalitarianism contrary to nature and good sense, completely upsets the domestic order.
>
> A garden therefore should be on several levels—the *jardin-potager*, the *jardin d'ornement* and the *jardin d'eau*.

And it is in this manner that the gardens of Villandry are laid out. Despite Dr Carvallo's rigid views the part of the garden which gives most pleasure is the lowest—both in terms of hierarchy and terrain—the *jardin-potager* or kitchen garden. The *jardin d'eau* on the highest level provides the irrigation for the rest of the garden. On the middle level to the south of the château the *jardin d'ornament* has beautifully maintained box *parterres* filled with flowers, symbolizing the different moods of love: fickle, tender, tragic and passionate.

The fascination of Villandry is the sheer variety and number of ways in which plants and trees are used to create architectural effects: the topiary, the trellised arbours, the clipped *allées* of lime, the box *parterres*, and in the *potager*, the edgings of low pleached apple. Each compartment in the *potager* is planted with different vegetables in carefully marshalled patterns and contrasting colours which change throughout the seasons.

All this is maintained currently by Madame Carvallo, wife of the original owner's grandson, and a team of seven gardeners, where once there were 50—witness to the fact that modern machinery such as machine-shears has made maintenance easier. At the entrance to the gardens is a map of the current year's planting, showing the thousands of plants bedded out each season.

Villandry is fascinating at any time of year, and has the special attraction that you can linger well after the last admission time and leave by a side door.

VILLESAVIN

Villesavin, it could be said, is like the roof of Chambord lifted off and placed on the ground. The steep roofs and elaborate dormers overwhelm the ground floor. The link is a real one for Villesavin's builder, Jean Le Breton, had shared François I's captivity at Pavia and acted as commissioner for the works at Chambord, a post assumed by his widow on his death in 1543.

Villesavin has no grand airs; it is a villa rather than a château. The entrance gates and lodges, swathed in ivy, are unkempt, and you do not see the house until you are right upon it.

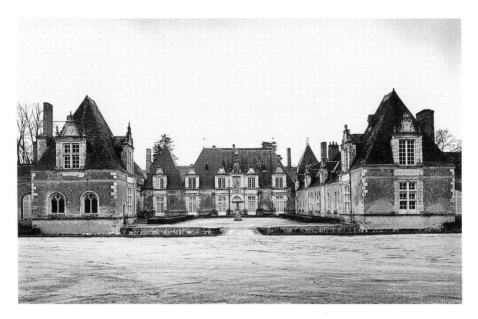

The *cour d'honneur* approached across a narrow moat (recently reopened), is flanked by service courts with engagingly exaggerated neo-Gothic entrances in red brick. Even on a dull day the gentle colour of the house is particularly appealing, like faded hide.

Villesavin: the *cour d'honneur* of the early 16th-century château.

Jean Le Breton acquired the property about 1527, and work must have been well advanced by 1536, the date on one of the dormers. These dormers are linked in vertical compositions to the window below and in the centre interestingly have the 1–3–1 grouping often characteristic of Italian Renaissance villas; they carry tapering tops, midway between gables and pediments, flanked by the usual candelabra. The ornamental carving is spirited though very worn and is being gradually renewed with great care. Currently just one-third of the roof of the *corps-de-logis* has been re-slated and the proprietor draws attention to the fact that he is still awaiting a promised state contribution to the remainder. Symmetry, it should be noted, is not perfect: the wing on the right is matched only by a screen wall opposite. Recent research shows the right-hand wing may have been the original *corps-de-logis*; certainly it contains some large fireplaces, today

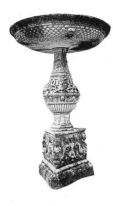

The Renaissance fountain in Villesavin's courtyard.

explained as a succession of kitchens (the first contains its ancient spit mechanism).

In the centre of the courtyard is a very fine marble urn, of a quality and scale that suggests it was commissioned from Genoa or Milan for the châteaux of Blois or Gaillon, but diverted here. It is also sometimes said to be a gift to Jean Le Breton by the sculptors working at Chambord.

The chapel in the entrance pavilion on the left has 16th-century murals that are strongly influenced by Italy. The paintings of the vault are 17th-century, ascribed to Jean Mosnier who worked at Cheverny. Looking onto the altar is an oratory with a rich cornice and *trompe-l'oeil* walls.

Behind the farm court (on the left) is a large and well-preserved dovecot with the original revolving oak ladder and 1,500 nesting-boxes. On the garden front one of the wings contains an orangery now equipped for receptions and parties. Here, the painted inscriptions date from the early 19th century, the period of the Marquis de Pradel, who had accompanied Louis XVIII to England as chamberlain.

The main rooms are not shown, but with their shuttered windows they heighten the sense of the *'belle aux bois dormants'*.

VOUZERON

Vouzeron has a special interest for the English visitor as its architect, Hippolyte Destailleur (1822–93) was the creator of the great Rothschild seat in Buckinghamshire, Waddesdon Manor (1874–80). Destailleur was on the international circuit, designing the town houses of Prince Pless in Berlin, and Albert de Rothschild in Vienna. Zestful is perhaps the best adjective to describe his work. Vouzeron is proof, if proof is still needed, that revival or pastiche can be spirited, inventive and exuberant.

The château is a strong cocktail of Flamboyant Gothic and Renaissance, executed in brick with substantial areas of stonework which flash brilliantly in the sun. The art lies in a gentle exaggeration: everything is a little more vertical and ornate than it would be in the original. The whole roof is of the same vertiginous steepness, and

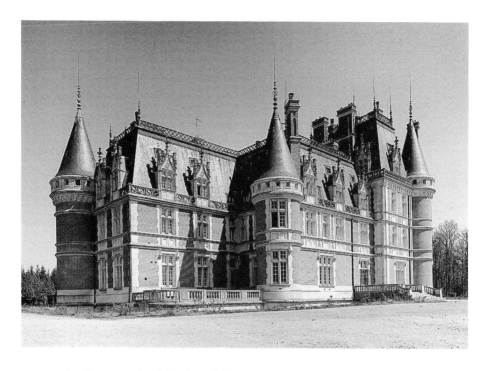

crowned all around with the richest of cresting and numerous spiky finials. The machicolations of the towers are inset in the Renaissance manner with sculpted shells, and the spirally-fluted lead rainwater pipes must be among the most ornamental ever fashioned. Inside, there is a massive staircase set in a hall of spectacular height.

The château stands on a terrace overlooking a lake; intriguingly no service buildings are in sight. But in the car park a subterranean entrance is visible with a narrow-gauge railway track for wheeling in supplies to the kitchens in the basement of the château. In the grounds, at a distance, are a series of appropriately elaborate estate buildings.

Today Vouzeron is a conference centre, impressively well run by the Fondation Ambroise-Croizat. The gates are just outside the town of the same name, on the road leading east. To reach Vouzeron, take the N 20 from Orléans to Salbris, then the D 944 to Neuvy-sur-Barangeon, and then the D 30 to Vouzeron.

The Château de la Triboulette at Vouzeron, an example of the late 19th-century Loire-revival style.

143

GLOSSARY

Arcade: series of arches supported on piers or columns.

Architrave: the lowest part of the classical *entablature*.

Baluster: vertical support of handrail, the whole being called the balustrade.

Capital: head or top of column.

Cartouche: a tablet with ornamental frame, often with scrollwork surround, sometimes containing a coat of arms.

Château fort: fortified castle.

Chemin-de-ronde: covered walk at top of castle tower or walk, usually rests on *machicolations*.

Coffering: sunken panels on ceiling or *vault*.

Collegiate church: one for the support of a college of priests, especially for the singing of masses for the soul of the founder.

Console: ornamental bracket.

Cornice: decorative moulding around top of building or room. Also the uppermost section of an *entablature*.

Corps-de-logis: the main building as distinct from the wings or pavilions.

Cresting: ornamental roof ridge usually of pierced leadwork.

Crockets: leaf-shaped ornamentation carved on sloping surfaces such as *dormer windows* and *pinnacles*.

Diaper: repeating pattern of brickwork, often a criss-cross of dark bricks on light.

Donjon: principal tower of a château or *château fort*; in early castles the equivalent of an English keep.

Dormer window: window standing out vertically from the slope of a roof.

Entablature: the moulded lintel carried by a classical column consisting traditionally of *architrave*, *frieze* and *cornice*.

Flamboyant: the last, most ornate phase of French Gothic.

Flèche: slender spire on centre of a roof.

Fleur-de-lis: formalized lily, as in royal arms of France.

Frieze: horizontal bands of ornament, especially middle section of classical *entablature*.

Garderobe: a medieval privy, or later a *chambre de toilette*.

Grotesque: literally grotto-esque, wall decoration of fanciful character.

Gunloop: opening in wall of tower, for gun or cannon.

Lantern: small turret crowning a roof, usually with windows.

Loggia: sheltered space behind a colonnade.

Lucarne: *dormer window*.

Lunette: semi-circular window.

Machicolations: battlements or wall-walks supported on corbels, with openings through which missiles can be dropped.

Order: one of the five classical orders – Tuscan, Doric, Ionic, Corinthian and Composite. A giant order fronts more than one storey.

Pediment: a triangular gable such as surmounted a classical temple.

Pendentive: area between arches supporting a dome.

Pilaster: flat version of a column, which projects very slightly from a wall.

Pinnacle: tapering finial on a buttress, *dormer* or parapet, sometimes decorated with *crockets*.

Portcullis: vertical gate that rises and falls in grooves at entrance to castle.

Porte cochère: main entrance porch large enough for wheeled vehicles to draw up and allow passengers to dismount under cover.

Portico: a large porch supported by freestanding columns.

Retable: altarpiece.

Reveal: inward slope of a window opening.

Scagliola: composite material imitating marble.

Term: pedestal tapering towards the base; it often supports a bust.

Vault: ceiling supported on arches and sometimes cross-ribs. Tunnel vaults or barrel vaults are rounded, without diagonal cross-ribs.

Voussoir: wedge-shaped stones which form an arch – that in the centre being the keystone.

SOME FURTHER READING

Babelon, Jean-Pierre, *Châteaux de la Renaissance Française*, Paris, 1989

Blomfield, Sir Reginald, *History of French Architecture 1494–1661*, London, 1911; *1661–1774*, London, 1921

Blunt, Anthony, *Art and Architecture in France 1500–1700*, London, 1970 (2nd ed.)

Braham, Allan and Smith, Peter, *François Mansart*, London, 1973

Collections Réalités, *Merveilles des Châteaux de la Loire*, Paris, 1964

Dunlop, Ian, *Châteaux of the Loire*, London, 1969

Editions de la Morande, *Châteaux et Demeures de l'Orléanais*
Chateaux et Manoirs du Blesois

Hautecoeur, Louis, *Histoire de l'Architecture Classique en France*, Paris, 1943 onwards

Knecht, Robert, *Francis I*, Cambridge, 1982

Montclos, Jean Marie Perouse de, *Architectures en Région Centre*, Paris, 1988

Monuments Historiques, Issue 164 (July-August 1989) on *Châteaux du Val de Loire*

Woodbridge, Kenneth, *Princely Gardens, the origin and development of the French formal garden style*, New York, 1986

Useful addresses

French Government Tourist Office, 178 Piccadilly, London W1V 0AL. Tel: (071) 491 7622.

Région Centre, Office du Tourisme, Pavillon Anne de Bretagne, 3 Avenue Dr Jean Laigret, 41000 Blois. Tel: (010 33) 54 74 06 49.

Tourisme de l'Anjou, BP2148, F49021 Angers, Cedex, France. Tel: (010 33) 41 88 23 85.

Contact the local tourist offices for details of *son et lumière* performances at the more famous châteaux, and also for information about lesser-known ones in the area.

CHRONOLOGY

CHÂTEAUX

SOME PRINCIPAL DATES

ANGERS	1230–40
LANGEAIS main period	1465–67
CHAUMONT west range	1465–75
south and east ranges	1498–1510
Louis XII wing at BLOIS	1498–1501
CHENONCEAU	1514–22
AZAY-LE-RIDEAU	1518–24
François I wing at BLOIS	1515–24
CHAMBORD	1519–24
	1526 onwards
BRISSAC	1606–21
CHEVERNY	1624–25
Gaston d'Orléans wing at BLOIS	1634–38
MONTGEOFFROY	1772–75
Pagoda at CHANTELOUP	1775
BONHÔTEL	1875–82
PONT-CHEVRON	1896–1900
VILLANDRY restoration of house	
and garden begun	1906

KINGS OF FRANCE

Louis IX, or Saint Louis	1226–70
Philippe III	1270–85
Philippe IV	1285–1314
Louis X	1314–16
Philippe V	1316–22
Charles IV	1322–28
Philippe VI	1328–50
Jean II	1350–64
Charles V	1364–80
Charles VI	1380–1422
Charles VII	1422–61
Louis XI	1461–83
Charles VIII	1483–98
Louis XII	1498–1515
François I	1515–47
Henri II	1547–59
François II	1559–60
Charles IX	1560–74
Henri III	1574–89
Henri IV	1589–1610
Louis XIII	1610–43

Louis XIV	1643–1715
Louis XV	1715–74
Louis XVI	1774–89
Napoleon I	1804–14
Louis XVIII	1814–24
Charles X	1824–30
Louis-Philippe	1830–48
Napoleon III	1852–70

ACKNOWLEDGEMENTS

Photographs
The publishers would particularly like to thank Colin Dixon for the special photography he undertook for this book.

Archives Département de Loir-et-Cher: 59; Arlaud/ © C.N.M.H.S./ S.P.A.D.E.M.: 89; Bibliothèque Nationale: 65, 132, 134; British Library: 41; J. Allan Cash: 47, 97; Keith Collie: 56; Conway Library, Courtauld Institute: 30, 43 (bottom), 55, 60, 74; Country Life: 104, 105; Colin Dixon: jacket photograph and pp. vi, 2, 4, 5, 8, 9, 10, 13, 17, 20, 23, 25, 28, 31, 33, 35, 37, 38, 40, 42, 43 (top), 44, 45, 48, 49, 52, 54, 57, 61, 63, 66, 67, 69, 70, 72, 76, 78, 79, 80, 82, 83, 84, 86, 88, 91, 92, 94, 100, 101, 107, 108, 110, 112, 114, 115, 116, 117, 119, 120, 121, 123, 125, 126, 128, 130, 131, 135, 136, 138, 139, 141, 142, 143; J. Feuillie/ © C.N.M.H.S./S.P.A.D.E.M.: 95; Association Henri et Achille Duchêne: 27; Giraudon, Musée Condé: 6; Robert Harding Picture Library: 109; Musées Nationaux: 102.

Plans
The following sources have provided the basis for certain maps and plans.
Hachette 135; D.A.C.S. 38; La Goélette, Paris (based on a plan by J.P. Conrad) 47; S.P.A.D.E.M: 129.
Every effort has been made to trace copyright-holders; it is hoped that any omission will be excused.

INDEX

INDEX